IN SEARCH OF DEMOCRACY IN SOCIALISM

HISTORY AND PARTY CONSCIOUSNESS

To pursue the breaking of the dialectic,
man himself must be broken.

—Maurice Merleau-Ponty

What, moreover, is that Self from which
man is alienated? It is the *homo ignotus* in
us which has not yet spread its wings. It is
the man who from the time of Spartacus to
the present day rises up against every kind
of oppression, not only economic. He must
at last rise to his proper stature.

—Ernst Bloch

IN SEARCH OF DEMOCRACY IN SOCIALISM

HISTORY AND PARTY CONSCIOUSNESS

svetozar stojanović
translated by gerson s. sher

₧ Prometheus Books
BUFFALO, NEW YORK 14215

Published 1981 by Prometheus Books
700 East Amherst Street, Buffalo, New York 14215

Library of Congress Catalog Number: 81-81130
ISBN: 0-87975-161-4

AUTHOR'S NOTE

The reader will probably observe that my new book is logically connected with my previous book, *Between Ideals and Reality: A Critique of Socialism and Its Future* (trans. Gerson S. Sher; New York: Oxford University Press, 1973), which was a translation of the Serbo-Croatian original published in Belgrade in 1969.

Everything that I have to say, I have written in the pages that follow. I have no intention of explaining the book in an Introduction. Some of the ideas that I have developed in the course of many years' work on the book have been extracted from contributions to various journals and anthologies. It would be inconsiderate for me to burden the reader with all the bibliographical details, since what is before him is a new text rather than a collection of published works.

In September 1977 I submitted the manuscript to two publishers: Prosveta (Belgrade) and Carl Hanser Verlag (Munich). My previous book had first been published in Belgrade, and then it appeared in translation in Germany and a number of other countries, including the U.S. Thus in the present case as well I wished to have my book appear first in my mother tongue. Unfortunately, to this day Prosveta has not been in a position, for political reasons, to give me any sort of definitive response. It would be senseless for me to go into all the details at this point since the reader will appreciate them for himself when he reads the book, particularly the sixth chapter in Part Two.

And thus, this book now appears in a second foreign language (the German edition was published in 1978 by Carl Hanser Verlag under the title, *Geschichte und Parteibewusstsein: Auf der Suche nach Demokratie im Sozializmus)* and is still inaccessible to the Yugoslav reader.

Svetozar Stojanović

December, 1980
Belgrade

CONTENTS

FOREWORD

As the author notes, this book was written in Yugoslavia, with the intention that it be published in Yugoslavia and read by a Yugoslav audience. This is not to say, however, that the book concerns are limited to the Yugoslav context, for in a general way they speak to one of the most profound problems of contemporary society: the role of the individual in the modern political organization. The enormous literature on this subject testifies to its great complexity, since it includes virtually every aspect of human existence: ethical, philosophical, economic, social, ideological, psychological, and what we commonly refer to, in its narrow sense as "political." In this work these concerns are focused onto one historical experience, that of the communist party organization of the Stalinist era.

No doubt there will be many who will object to any suggestion that Stalin's Communist Party — or more generally, in the author's usage, the "Stalinized communist party," a term that extents to those communist political organizations of other countries that adopted the Stalinist model — should be viewed as the exemplary political organization of the twentieth century, much less the Great Terror of the Soviet 1930s as the paragon of political conduct. Nor is this the author's purpose, stated or implied. Yet in a sense what is depicted here can be read as the most extreme historical development of a notion deriving from Marx's early writings, "political alienation," the rule of man's political institutions over men and women as a disembodied, hostile, and alien force. Under Stalinism this was particularly poignant in the case of the relationship between the party's original founders, who had joined it as a political organization dedicated to revolutionary change, and the party itself, which became transformed into a bureaucratic organization dedicated to the needs of a new bureaucratic class and to the perpetuation of its rule. The Old Bolsheviks, accused of betraying the organization that they helped to build, were ultimately all but exterminated by it. It is they who were the principal casualties of Stalin's terror.

Why, however, should these issues be raised by a Yugoslav philosopher nearly a half-century later? Had not the horrors of Stalinism been thoroughly laid open to view in the intervening years—in part, indeed, by the official Yugoslav critique of the Soviet political system and in part by the writings of Yugoslav apostates, such as Milovan Djilas? And what is the relevance of Stalinism to Yugoslav society today?

If this book is read not so much as an historical exposé of the Stalinist system but as a critique of the Stalinist political mentality from a Marxist-humanist perspective, then the answer to the last question will be, a great deal. For it has long been the author's contention that despite the organizational changes and the on-again-off-again openness to internal criticism that have marked its history since the early 1950s, the League of Communists of Yugoslavia retains many of the characteristics of a traditional communist party of the Stalinist mold. Beginning in the early 1960s the author, at the time a member of the LCY, sought to advance the argument that the League needed to make greater provision for the rights of the minority in the intra-party discussion and policy-making and that the notion of "democratic centralism"—which had been introduced by Lenin but perverted by Stalin into an instrument of blind autocratic obedience—needed to be interpreted more liberally, with greater emphasis on the democratic component. An institution in which the "unity of thought" was the absolute precondition of the "unity of action" was, he maintained, unfit to serve as the organizational model of a truly democratic socialist society. This position was roundly rejected by the political leadership, and their suggestions that the League of Communists had no place for such individuals was instrumental in persuading the author and several other prominent Yugoslav thinkers to found their own journal of critical, Marxist theory— *Praxis*—in 1964.[1]

These events marked only the beginning of the author's personal encounter with the authoritarian legacy of Stalinism in Yugoslav political life. Unremitting in his forthright and radical (in the Marxist sense: "to grasp things by the root") criticism of statism and authoritarianism in contemporary socialist society and in identifying the shortcomings of the Yugoslav system of self-management in practice as opposed to its ideal potential, he continued to provoke sharp criticism by the League's house theoreticians and was the target of many a hostile article in the official press. When in 1968 the students of Belgrade

University took to the streets to protest conditions ranging from social privilege and inequality to poor housing, he and his colleagues at the Department of Philosophy were branded as the scapegoats and their Party memberships were summarily revoked. From that time forth Tito waged a personal campaign against them, demanding their dismissal from the University as morally and politically unfit to guide the nation's youth, although remarkably he was unable to bring his efforts to fruition until 1975. In January of that year the Serbian Parliament, acting on the basis of a law of dubious constitutionality passed a few months before, suspended the author and seven other Belgrade philosophy professors from their duties. This decision was appealed but to no avail, and for the next six years they were placed on half-salary by the Serbian Ministry of Culture pending their location of other jobs.[2] In the meantime they were subjected to continued public attacks without any right of reply, forced to seek temporary work elsewhere (some, including the author, accepted occasional visiting teaching appointments abroad), and were treated for all purposes as second-class citizens. Finally, in 1981 they were dismissed outright from the University in a demonstration by the post-Tito regime of its continued intolerance of dissent and its obsession with unity at all costs.

It will perhaps be pointed out that if this is the legacy of Stalinism, then Stalinism has certainly become relatively benign over the years. At least until very recently, the Belgrade professors had passports, state salaries, freedom to teach abroad, and even in some cases the ability to write theoretical articles for publication in Yugoslavia. Even their dismissal from Belgrade University is surely a far cry from Siberia or the prison institutes of Solzhenitsyn's Russia, or for that matter from Goli otok and the harsh imprisonment or exile of many other Yugoslav dissidents who may not have shared the *Praxis* philosophers' Marxist credentials or scholarly reputations.[3] What, then, does this have in common with Stalinism?

The answer, I believe, is twofold. First, if we accept the notion of Stalinism as, in the Weberian sense, an "ideal type" of communist authoritarianism, then we are speaking of a system of value and a pattern of conduct which may be more or less pronounced in given historical instances but possessed of an inherent cultural continuity and persistence that is exceedingly difficult to root out. The source of this Stalinist political culture in the case of Yugoslavia is a matter of historical record, for the "Bolshevization" (read "Stalinization") of the Yugoslav Communist Party was carried out in the late 1930s by Tito himself and it was this new Party, with Tito and his select leadership at the helm, that brought the new Yugoslavia into being, through the fires of the Partisan War, the struggle with Stalin in the late 1940s, the purge of the "Cominformists," and, to be sure, the introduction of a new and potentially democratic type of socialist organization, workers' self-management. In this process the Party itself underwent many changes, some of them designed to allow greater discussion and observance of democratic norms in its ranks. But were these steps sufficient to eliminate authoritarian habits of thought and action in the Party leadership, or even in the rank and file? This is an important question that bears vitally on the ability of communist regimes to reform themselves internally, and the present work is a provocative attempt to deal with it in the Yugoslav context.

The second reason is of a more personal nature. In this book the author devotes considerable attention to the dignity of the revolutionary and his conduct toward his own party when accused by it of deviant activity. The true revolutionary does not have the moral right, we are told, to sacrifice his dignity, nor does the truly revolutionary party have the moral right to demand this sacrifice and indeed defeats its own purpose if it does. For once the personal dignity of the revolutionary is allowed to become an instrument of collective discipline, the downhill slide toward the depths of human depravity found in the full-blown Stalinism has begun. This is why, for instance, the author's historical account of Stalinism in the USSR focuses more closely on the first public recantations of the anti-Stalinist opposition of the mid 1920s than on the more spectacular forced confessions of the late 1930s. And in his own struggle against party authoritarianism, it perhaps explains why he and his colleagues considered their refusal to accept as final their suspension from Belgrade University a matter of high moral principle more than a merely personal *point d'honneur.* Despite their expulsion from the Party in 1968, despite their vilification in the official press as "enemies of self-management," and despite the personal hardships they have suffered in particular since 1975, the Belgarde *Praxis* professors have retained their humanistic commitment to Marxism and the goals of democratic socialism, much as they may have become bitterly disenchanted with the institutional forms that these have assumed.

It is with the institutional forms of contemporary socialism, and with the ideological mentality that underlies them, that this book is primarily concerned. One of the earliest and, in the Marxist literature, best-known attempts to address these issues and to relate them in a systematic manner was made by György Lukács, who, toward the end of his *History and Class Consciousness* (1919-1922), undertook a theoretical defense of the Leninist model of political organization as applied to the immediate post-revolutionary situation. It is evident that the present work, with its closely parallel subtitle of *History and Party Consciousness,* is meant by the author to begin, in a sense, where Lukács left off. It was Lukács who, prior to the discovery of the explicitly humanistic manuscripts of the young Marx, brilliantly reconstructed Marxist theory to emphasize the active, conscious role of the human subject in the making of history and to lay in philosophical ruin the super-deterministic perspective that had come to dominate the dogma of the Second International. All this is fully consistent with the thrust of the philosophical argument in the first part of the present book, except that its author (I believe accurately) argues that Marx's own writings were ambiguous on the issue of historical determinism and partly responsible for the ensuing theoretical confusion.

But on the subject of revolutionary organization, there was much in Lukác's presentation that was lacking and indeed misleading. In his essay "Towards a Methodology of the Problem of Organisation," Lukács seems to have made the crucial mistake of failing to distinguish between what he saw as the party's ideal potential and its real form. Thus we find Lukács, for whom the party was "the concrete mediation between man and history,"[4] insisting that party discipline involves "the unconditional absorption of the total personality in the praxis of the movement" and that "only through discipline can the party be capable of putting the collective will into practice" even as he warned, in the case of the Bolshevik Party, against "the dangers of ossification, bureaucratisation and corruption."[5] For Lukács the elements of discipline and unity were but part of a totality of revolutionary activity which, in the form of the party, was to serve as an instrument for forging a truly coherent proletarian class consciousness through its historical praxis.

Sixty years later, however, the overriding issue has become, in the present author's view, not so much the consciousness of the class but precisely that of the Party, which, as has so often been pointed out by both its internal and external critics, has ceased to exist for the proletariat but exists rather for the sake of preserving its own dominant position in society. In this context, the issue of discipline and the total submersion of the individual personality in the Party's "collective will" are posed in a totally different light. To be sure, these problems were apparent to many of Lukács's contemporaries too, among them Rosa Luxemburg, whom he took explicitly to task for her skepticism over Lenin's organizational methods. But while it may still be arguable whether Lenin's methods or Stalin's perversion of them were ultimately responsible for the ensuing human tragedy, it is clear that the result bears little resemblance to the vision sketched out by Lukács in the early days of the Bolshevik regime. In a sense, then, this book is an attempt to recast the terms of the debate with the undeniable advantage of hindsight—which, however, as the author's fate only reminds us, is not always received with gratitude by those whose narrow vision condemns them to repeat the mistakes of the past in the present.

Gerson S. Sher
January 1981

NOTES

1. On the *Praxis* movement and the author's role in it, see my *Praxis: Marxist Criticism and Dissent in Socialist Yugoslavia* (Bloomington: Indiana University Press, 1977).
2. One of the original eight suspended professors did accept a job elsewhere in Yugoslavia.

3. This is not to say that Marxists have been immune from imprisonment in Yugoslavia, nor all the *Praxis* group for that matter (Mihailo Djurić and Božidar Jakšić). But the burden has fallen much more heavily on other groups, such as the nationalist "right," outright terrorists, and the occasional pro-Soviet party-cell-in-hiding.
4. Georg Lukács, *History and Class Consciousness,* trans. Rodney Livingstone (London: Merlin, 1971), p. 318.
5. *Ibid.,* pp. 316, 320, 335.

Part One
Marxism and Historical Action

1. The Approach to Marx

The longstanding controversy over Marx's intellectual development has led to more profound study of his work. Thanks to this, the claim that there is a humanistic continuity in Marx's thought is today firmly grounded.

Not even Althusser, the most capable defender of the thesis of Marx's "epistemological break," has succeeded in bringing this claim seriously into question. What is actually involved in Althusser is a new version of an old interpretation of Marx. The difference lies mainly in the fact that Althusser's intellectual apparatus — in part deriving from contemporary structuralism, epistemology, psychoanalysis, and linguistics — is more developed and modern and his mode of argument somewhat clearer. But even he is forced to acknowledge that in the works of Marx's "complete maturity" (1857 onward) — not to mention his "maturation period" (1845 to 1857) — there are significant elements that link those works with his pre-1845 writings. In spite of this Althusser has no doubts as to the existence of two Marxes, one opposed to the other: the first an ideologist, a humanist, and a Hegelian, and the second — once he had matured — a scientist, a theoretical antihumanist, and an anti-Hegelian. Everything that does not fit with his interpretation Althusser "symptomatically" proclaims to be a "remnant" of Marx's prescientific, ideological, humanist phase. But of what sort of "epistemological break" can one seriously speak when there are so many "remnants" of such significance of the preceding phase?! It is worth adding that even in his *Eléments d'autocritique* (1974) Althusser does not retreat from the view of Marx described above.

But if there are not two Marxes divided by an "epistemological break," can the truth be grasped in the simple counter-assertion that there is *one* Marx? Let us not dodge the issue, for a good deal of the current literature on Marx stresses the homogeneity of his opus. I do not have in mind here so much the fact that Marx's humanistic thought, in the process of maturation, became more radical (the path from liberal to revolutionary) and concrete (the transcendence of an abstract anthropological perspective by a more historically and scientifically grounded approach). Since it is well known that with the course of time Marx broadened his thematic horizons and modified his sphere of interest and his emphases, this is not what concerns me. But in addition to the myth of two completely different Marxes, there is also the danger of constructing a monolithic mythology of Marx. For Marx's interpreters have often projected their own politically and ideologically monolithic notions onto Marx himself.

Since the mid-1950s there has been a true eruption of humanistic Marxism, even in certain countries in which Marxism is the official ideology—above all in Yugoslavia, Poland, and Hungary. There has developed an anti-Stalinist theoretical movement which goes by the watchword, "Back to the true Marx." But as I have said, we must eschew two, not one, myths about Marx. Thus a truly creative return to his opus must be selective and critical.

My previous book was written in this spirit. There I devoted a good deal of attention to the examination of various tensions and contradictions in Marx's intellectual edifice. But I treated them as differences *between* individual levels— metatheories, abstractly formulated theories, and theories that were applied in the course of research—rather than *within* those levels. I begin this book with a consideration of the tension between Marx's strict and tempered determinism, as well as that between economistic schemes and the economic approach to history in his work.

2. The Contradiction Between Strict and Tempered Determinism

The past few decades have witnessed the rapid development of a new philosophical discipline in the Anglo-Saxon countries—the theory of action. The first generation of analysts of actions was *reductionist:* it considered that the language of human action could be translated into causal language. The more recent generation has a *teleological* point of view. In contrast to cause-and-effect phenomena, they reason, human action cannot be explained unless motives are taken into account. And motives, be they social rules or the actors' goals, cannot be interpreted in any sense as causes, no matter how unique they might otherwise be.

In the analytical theory of action a good deal of valuable time has been squandered, moreover, in reductionist errors. This is a price that is commonly paid for the existence of several mutually, totally closed universes within a new philosophy. Had they been sufficiently mindful of European continental— especially German—philosophy, the analysts of action would have seen that an entire constellation of significant philosophers persuasively opposed positivistic efforts to describe the world of man and his action by means of a conceptual apparatus borrowed from the natural sciences. Here I have in mind, of course, the philosophy of life, neo-Kantianism, hermeneutics, phenomenology, or individuals such as Droysen, Dilthey, Windelband, Simmel, Weber, etc. Some of them dug an unbridgeable chasm between the *explanation* of natural activities and the *understanding* of human ones. Nevertheless, it bears remembering that continental philosophy for its part has not followed the evolution of the Anglo-Saxon theory of action closely enough. The latter's depth and precision of *logical* analysis would certainly have something of value to contribute to the continental school.

* * *

How does Marx's thought look in the light of the problematic that concerns the analysts of action? Can Marx, moreover, help us in discovering the limitations of their position? For our purposes here it will be sufficient to respond to these questions in schematic form.

Marxism arose as a unique and radical theory of action. All the more strange is it that not a single significant Marxist has attempted to construct a *systematic* approach to action. In contrast to his vulgar interpreters and followers, Marx had a *teleological* understanding of action. Marx's conception of action, like all others, was founded on a specific understanding of man. I would underestimate the reader's erudition were I at this point to resort to quotations, beginning with the familiar passages in the first volume of *Capital* in which an essential distinction is drawn between the "labor" of bees and that of man. One of the most important components of Marx's philosophical and scientific outlook is his definition of man as a practical being who establishes goals.

Man as actor influences the nature of being in every respect, according to Marx. The domain of human activity is far smaller, for instance, for Wittgenstein:

> If the good or bad exercise of the will does alter the world, it can alter only the limits of the world, not the facts—not what can be expressed by means of language. In short the effect must be that it becomes an altogether different world. It must, so to speak, wax and wane as a whole. [1]

Marx's ultimate goal is not the comprehension of action as such, but a mode of action itself (Eleventh Thesis on Feuerbach). When a Marxist begins to study the analytical theory of action, one of the first things to strike him is its self-imposed contemplative nature.

Some of the other internal impediments of the theory are presented as follows by Richard Bernstein in his excellent book, *Praxis and Action:*

> Many different lines of inquiry in analytical philosophy have brought us to an appreciation of how deeply man's language and action is embedded in and conditioned by social practices and institutions. We cannot even begin to make sense of what we mean by action unless we consider how specific instances of actions are embodied in the social practices and institutions that shape our lives. This has not only been a central motif in recent analytical philosophy, it is central to Hegel, Marx, and the pragmatists. But in the past, analytic philosophers have not pressed their inquiries concerning the social context of action and practice. They have not paid much attention to the dynamics of social change and to the factors that shape those practices and institutions which are the medium of our lives. Nor have they paid much attention to the critical question of what ought to be the direction of social change. The biases which once existed against considering such issues as legitimate philosophic questions no longer carry much conviction. . . . In short, some younger analytic philosophers are bringing to their investigation a sense of history, development, and social change that has too frequently been lacking in analytic work.[2]

Although a teleologist by his point of departure, Marx was drawn immeasurably more to the external, objective aspect of action than to its internal and subjective side. At the focus of his interest is the process of objectification, particularly in the form of socio-historical actions and institutions. Marx utilized the concepts of intention, motive, goal, desire, reason, choice, decision, and so forth, but he did not submit them to logical analysis. This task has been skillfully accomplished by certain contemporary analytical thinkers. The Marxist must search for his truly creative opportunity in the development of Marx's concepts, such as need, ability, praxis, alienation, reification, fetishization, and so on. In this regard the perspective revealed through the essential connectedness between Marxism's understanding of action and its philosophy of society and history must be seen as a significant advantage. The meaning of human acts as defined by the actors' intentions and motives figures in the Marxist jargon as "subjective meaning." Marxists, in contrast, are oriented from the start toward "objective meaning," and this meaning is comprised of the consequences of action.

For Marx man defines himself *only* by *what he does.* The concrete and real nature of any individual's goals is revealed even to the executor only in practice. In this transition from subjective to objective meaning can be found the counterbalance to the inclination toward (self-)deception, which in the life of social groups assumes the form of ideology. But caution: man is that which *truly does,* but man is not to be identified with that which *happens to action unpredictably and beyond his control.* Analytical thinkers call this the distinction between "doing" and "happening." In Marx's language, this can partly be termed a distinction between the unalienated and unreified dimension of human action, as opposed to the alienated and reified dimension.

Even the most individual act is played out in a social context. Intentions and actions overtake, intersect, intertwine, permeate, stimulate, or cancel the intentions and actions of other people. This often leads to an enormous variance between intentions and results. Human actions are included in a whole whose significance transcends their meaning taken individually. The result of action—its objective meaning, as Hegelians and Marxists would say—is formed only in interaction. The actor cannot avoid *interactor-ness.* In passing I might say that for a Marxist intersubjectivity is primarily an aspect of interactor-ness, rather than the reverse. The outcome of action, not infrequently, is and at the same time is not the expression, the objectification, of the actor. There are different degrees, to be sure, of this alienation of effect: unintended, unforeseen, unforeseeable, unavoidable. On these truths are founded the great moments of mythology, literary tragedy, and the philosophy of history (of a Vico or a Hegel).

This picture is further complicated when we introduce collective actors and the historical dimension. An extraordinary illustration can be found in Engels' *Peasant War in Germany.* Sartre has found in Marx's and Engels' discussions important inspirations for his efforts in his *Critique of Dialectical Reason* to work out a Marxist theory of group actors.

One might complete this compilation simply by mentioning the problem of "impersonal forces" in history which, of course, are nothing other than the alienated consequences of numerous—often anonymous—individual and group projects.

* * *

And thus we circuitously arrive at an idea of importance in establishing the character of Marx's determinism: the "naturalness" *(Naturhaftigkeit)* of the previous course of history. In order to avoid a potential misunderstanding it should be recalled that for Marx historical existence is otherwise *un-natural* in the sense that it is of a developmental character rather than being cyclical as many thinkers, particularly classical, had maintained. It is clear, then, that the "naturalness" of the historical process in the context of this discussion refers to something other than its cyclical character.

Here we have reference to an aspect of Engels which cannot be neglected. I cite him first because it was only under his influence that Marx began to make use of the idea of the "naturalness" of previous history:

This law with its constant adjustment, in which whatever is lost here is gained there, is regarded as something excellent by the economist. It is his chief glory — he cannot see enough of it, and considers it in all its possible and impossible applications. Yet it is obvious that this law is purely a law of nature and not a law of the mind. It is a law which produces revolution. The economist comes along with his lovely theory of demand and supply, proves to you that "one can never produce too much," and practice replies with trade crises, which reappear as regularly as the comets, and of which we have now on the average one every five to seven years.[3]

Occasionally Engels presents a somewhat weaker thesis, not about the *total* *"naturalness"* of the socio-historical process, but rather drawing a *strong analogy* between it and existence in nature:

In the second place, however, history is made in such a way that the final result always arises from conflicts between many individual wills, of which each in turn has been made what it is by a host of particular conditions of life. Thus there are innumerable intersecting forces, an infinite series of parallelograms of forces which give rise to one resultant — the historical event. This may again itself be viewed as the product of a power which works as a whole *unconsciously* and without volition. For what each individual wills is obstructed by everyone else, and what emerges is something that no one willed. *Thus history has proceeded hitherto in the manner of a natural process and is essentially subject to the same laws of motion.*[4]

Yet those who ascribe naturalistic determinism to Engels alone and not to Marx are mistaken. For Marx approvingly quoted a reviewer of *Capital* who wrote: "*Marx treats the social movement as a process of natural history,* governed by laws not only independent of human will, consciousness, and intelligence, but rather, on the contrary, determining that will, consciousness, and intelligence. . ."[5]

Here is another passage in the same spirit:

It requires a fully developed production of commodities before, from accumulated experience alone, the scientific conviction springs up, that all the different kinds of private labour, which are carried on independently of each other, and yet as spontaneously developed branches of the social division of labour, are continually being reduced to the quantitative proportions in which society requires them. And why? Because, in the midst of all the accidental and ever fluctuating exchange-relations between the products, the labour-time socially necessary for their production forcibly asserts itself *like an over-riding law of Nature. The law of gravity thus asserts itself when a house falls about our ears.*[6]

Of special interest is this passage: "Intrinsically, it is not a question of the higher or lower degree of development of the social antagonisms that result from the *natural laws* of capitalist production. It is a question of these *laws* themselves, of *these tendencies* working with *iron necessity* towards inevitable results."[7] Here Marx presents a naturalistic determinism according to which social laws function like "natural laws" with "iron necessity," but at the same time a substantially milder determinism in which these laws are only tendencies. The latter leaves sufficient room for the influence of human activity. In this conflicting understanding of social laws, the difference between the social science of the nineteenth and twentieth centuries is already anticipated in schematic form. Many works which interpret the laws of capitalism in a statistical manner might be strengthened by affirming the existence of a more tempered determinism in Marx's work. One illustration will suffice: "The assumption that the commodities of the various spheres of production are sold at their value merely implies, of course, that their value is the center of gravity around which their prices fluctuate, and their continual rises and drops tend to equalise."[8]

It is generally recognized, however, that "naturalness," according to Marx and Engels, is not an *inevitable* property of history. Associated humanity will be in a position to transcend this realm of necessity and to bring an end to prehistory by establishing the realm of freedom as the form of true history.

Marx translated the alienated and reified dimension of action into naturalistic-causal language. But did it not, in fact, turn out that his point of departure was teleological?! The fact of the matter is that Marx was, in a certain sense, *both a teleologist and a causalist,* for he attempted to capture the paradoxical nature of human activity and the human situation. Although action is goal-oriented from the standpoint of the actor, in its *cumulative effects* — particularly in collective interaction and on the historical plane — it can often be grasped by means of causal-naturalistic categories. The dialectic manifests itself here in the sense that actions transform themselves into their opposite: although they are teleological taken individually, nevertheless the socio-historical process is of a causal-naturalistic character. Socio-historical motion heretofore has not had the property of praxis (conscious, free, and coordinated collective goal-orientedness).

The problem lies more in the duality of human action described above than in the dualistic nature of Marx's thought noted by G. H. von Wright in his famous book, *Explanation and Understanding:* "The point of view which Marx represents demonstrates an obvious dualism between the 'causalistic' and 'scientistic' orientation, on the one hand, and the 'hermeneutical dialectic' and 'teleological' orientation on the other."[9]

I cannot let this opportunity pass without alluding to one other aspect of the dialectic of human goal-orientedness. The question involves the degree to which the actor establishes goals in a truly free and self-determining manner, as opposed to the extent to which those goals are the consequence of habit, routine, training, and manipulation. When the latter is the case, is it not necessary to speak of action more as *consequence* than as goal-oriented? This apparent or pseudo-goal-orientedness represents one of the modes of alienation, reification, and indeed the "naturalness" of human action.

* * *

It is sensible to speak in terms of the "naturalness" of the socio-historical process insofar as that process has heretofore unfolded beyond the control of people, behind their backs. Man does create history, but in an alienated manner. More precisely, a small number of people consciously build history, a greater number are drawn into the process of creation, while the majority is simply cast into the bloody maelstrom and the mainstream of history and indeed experiences it as natural disaster or even catastrophe. More happens to them than they *do*. A vivid example along these lines was given by Marx in writing of the Roman slaves as the passive pedestal of historical conflict. Of many historical phenomena, such as wars and revolutions, it is properly said that they break out rather than being created by any specific person.

This manner of experiencing the motion of history as natural spontaneity was expressed in the ideas of Marx and Engels on the "naturalness" of the previous course of social development. The spontaneous, anarchic character of the capitalist economy (*laissez-faire* in many senses) of their time strengthened them in their belief. To be sure, modern capitalism differs in many respects, but despite efforts to subdue economic ferment it still bears the mark of a rather uncontrolled process.

It is true that Marx and Engels were guilty of some exaggeration, for not only did they draw an analogy between natural and social events and laws, they also occasionally conceptualized the latter on the model of the former. It is accurate to say that in society and in history certain types of behavior, interaction, and relationships demonstrate a kind of regularity that can be characterized as lawful. From the philosophy of science, however, we know that certain characteristics divide nomic statements in the social and historical sciences from those in the natural sciences.

Social and historical laws, more than natural laws, are valid only under strictly defined and multifaceted conditions. Moreover, the former are also relative in the sense that they change, whereas the latter are valid *semper et ubique*, as G. H. von Wright might put it. Marx undoubtedly was aware of this as well: "No natural laws can be done away with. What can change is only the *form* in which these laws assert themselves."[10] And no reasonably complete list of particulars could fail to note that social laws are, as a rule, tendentious and statistical in character.

Why, then, was Marx nevertheless convinced that there exist "natural" laws of socio-historical development? First of all, he was deeply impressed with the results of the natural sciences and took them to be the paradigm of all scientific endeavor. For this reason it is justified to ascribe an element of positivism to him. And indeed Marx contributed to this interpretation by the manner in which he understood his entire work. There is not an author who would not, in this context, cite Marx's statement in *The German Ideology* that from the territory of speculation he had passed over into the area of real, positive science.

Another influence on Marx consisted of the fact that some of the leading economists on whom he critically relied also had attempted to discover laws which, in their main characteristics, would be identical to those of natural sciences. Of course there was also the substantial influence of Hegel, with his strict historical determinism. Also, in order to distinguish himself from the utopians, Marx attempted to ground his socialism in science. He considered, unhappily, that this obliged him to demonstrate that the fall of capitalism and its succession by socialism was not only a historical possibility and tendency, but a "natural necessity."

It was only several decades later that strict determinism would enter into an irreversible crisis in the natural sciences as well, with the revolutionary discoveries of microphysics. From this we know that in a good part of the natural sciences, too, laws describe only average statistical tendencies. From historical experience it is also known today that new armaments and the possibility of ecological catastrophe have generated a situation in which not only progress, but the existence of mankind, is not guaranteed, not to mention the necessity of socialism.

* * *

There are some who accuse Marx of both reifying the historical process and elevating history to the level of a separate subject and actor. Among these are also critics who do not wish to treat these charges separately. To the extent to which Marx found "natural" laws and necessities in history rather than mere similarities to them, it is possible to speak of the reification of history on his part. The second charge against Marx's soul, however, consists merely of the sins of certain of his followers. Under Stalinism, for example, real people and events disappeared from the Marxist understanding of history, leaving hypostatized abstractions such as the forces of production and the relations of production, the economic base and social superstructure, classes and class conflict, etc.

In *The Holy Family* severe criticism is directed against the position which holds that "*history* thus becomes, like *truth*, a separate entity, a metaphysical subject of which the real human individuals are only mere representatives."[11] Stalinized historical materialism commits the same kind of error, with the difference that in the role of the estranged subject it replaces Hegel's Spirit with the development of the forces of production and the relations of production.

Marx disassociated himself in advance from followers of this sort. "History," he wrote, "does *nothing*. . . . *It is men,* real, living men, who do all this, who possess things and fight battles. It is not 'history' which uses men as a means of achieving – as if it were an individual person – *its* own ends. History is *nothing* but the activity of men in pursuit of their ends."[12] Or as Marx wrote on another occasion:

> History is nothing but the succession of the separate generations, each of which exploits the materials, the capital funds, the productive forces handed down to it by all preceding generations, and thus, on the one hand, continues the traditional activity in completely changed circumstances and, on the other, modifies the old circumstances with a completely changed activity.[13]

In conclusion, no one can deny that Marx explicitly asserted that man himself is a productive force, and indeed the most important productive force in the course of history.

What, then, is the source of the impression that Marx conferred on history the role of a separate subject and actor? Not, as we have seen, merely his own manner of speaking. What is more important in this regard is that according to Marx, the course of history is independent of the consciousness, intentions, and will of people. But it is then commonly overlooked that this independent course of history is in fact the result of interactor-ness and intersubjectivity (to be sure, unconscious and uncoordinated), and not of some "history" which, like the Hegelian Spirit, constitutes its own efficient and final cause. In other words, Marx did not utilize Feuerbach's transformational method in the critique of Hegel's system merely in order to consummate his own particular mystification of history. History, according to Marx, is not a subject and actor but the predicate and result of the collective activity of people. Man is the sole maker of history, but his product is alienated from him.

3. Economistic Schemes

We can best appreciate how important theoretical ideas can acquire schematic characteristics by referring to the familiar extract from Marx's Preface to *A Contribution to the Critique of Political Economy*. It is so well known that there is no need to quote it. However elastically and sympathetically we may read that text, we must conclude that Marx was speaking of a strict parallel between the development of the forces of production and the relations of production (in which the forces of production are the determining factor), as well as positing a unidirectional dependence of the legal-political and intellectual superstructure on the economic base.

Therefore I cannot agree with Habermas when he states, in an important essay, that the thesis about Marx's economism is the fruit of a misunderstanding:

This theorem about base and superstructure is often mistakenly understood in an economistic sense. From the context in which Marx poses the theorem it follows, however, with complete clarity that he wished to affirm the dependence of the superstructure on the base only for those critical phases in which a society passes over into a new stage of development. There is no question here of the *ontological organization* of society, but rather of the *leading role assumed by the economic structure in social evolution.* [14]

Yet the formulation of the question by Marx in his "Preface" is hardly unique. Here are a few more passages in which the social process is compressed into the economistic scheme of base and superstructure:

M. Proudhon the economist has clearly understood that men make cloth, linen, and silk stuffs in definite relations of production. But what he has not understood is that these definite social relations are just as much produced by men as are the cloth, the linen, etc. Social relations are intimately bound up with productive forces. *In acquiring new productive forces men change their mode of production, and in changing their mode of production, their manner of making a living, they change all their social relations. The windmill gives you society with the feudal lord; the steam mill, society with the industrial capitalist. The same men who established social relations in conformity with their material productivity also produce principles, ideas, and categories conforming to their social relations.* [15]

And a bit further Marx writes:

Is not this as much as saying that the mode of production, the relations in which productive forces are developed, are anything but eternal laws but that they correspond to a specific development of men and their productive forces, and that a *change arising in men's productive forces necessarily leads to a change in their relations of production?* [16]

4. The Transcendence of Economism

The truth is also, however, that in their *concrete* investigations of societies, phenomena, and events, Marx and Engels transcended these economistic schemes. Faced with the complexity of historical life, the schemes had to yield. This is witnessed not only by numerous passages from individual works, but also by entire writings, such as *The Class Struggles in France* and *The Eighteenth Brumaire of Louis Bonaparte.* Any inquiry which does not draw a distinction between the abstract and the operative theory of base and superstructure thoroughly misses the mark.

As an investigator Marx was far, for example, from reducing his explanation of historical phenomena to the conflict of two basic classes. Thus in his analysis of *The Class Struggles in France* we find six class groupings, and in *Revolution and Counterrevolution in Germany* no less than nine. Moreover, Marx often conceded a substantially more independent role to the state and political factors in general than might follow from his economistic formulae. It is common knowledge that this scheme was derived from study of the bourgeois societies of the West, in which the ruling political position of the bourgeoisie flowed from its economic predominance. In contrast, however, Marx's analysis of the "Asiatic mode of production" seems not to exclude the assumption that the political power of the state was an autonomous factor and even the source of its dominant economic power.

Marx also repeatedly stressed that the production of material goods and other human pursuits are *mutually* conditioned. For example:

> Man himself is the basis of his material production, as of all production which he accomplishes. All circumstances, therefore, which affect man, the *subject* of production, have a greater or lesser influence upon all his functions and activities, including his functions and activities as the creator of material wealth, of commodities. In this sense, it can truly be asserted that all human relations and functions, however and wherever they manifest themselves, influence material production and have a more or less determining effect upon it.[17]

It is well known that even during Marx's lifetime, many of his followers had begun to give primacy to the economistic schemes. In order to keep them at a healthy distance from Marx and himself, Engels was in the habit of saying:

> Marx and I are ourselves partly to blame for the fact that the younger people sometimes lay more stress on the economic side than is due to it. We had to emphasize the main principle vis-à-vis our adversaries, who denied it, and we had not always the time, the place, or the opportunity to give their due to the other elements involved in the interaction. But when it came to presenting a section of history, that is, to making a practical appiication, it was a different matter and there no error was permissible.[18]

It is hard to disagree with Engels that he and Marx were partly guilty for the fact that Marxists had begun to succumb to economism. However, the reason for this did not simply lie in the insufficiency of time, place, or opportunity to "give their due" to the *mutual* interaction of the economic base and the social superstructure. The fact is that the economistic scheme was attributed to Marx and Engels not without some justification. It is present in their writings, here and there, in all its severity—to be sure, often in a polemical context and form. I find it strange, therefore, that in his *Critique of Dialectical Reason* Sartre ascribes the full responsibility to Engels, while leaving Marx totally unscathed.

When Engels says, "according to the materialist conception of history, the *ultimately* determining element in history is the production and reproduction of real life," immediately adding that "more than this neither Marx nor I have ever asserted,"[19] he is simply not telling the whole truth, for there are unquestionably passages where their thesis is far more strongly stated.

In stressing this point I certainly do not mean to vindicate Marx's and Engels' economistic vulgarizers. After all, Engels did go to great lengths to disassociate himself from such interpretations:

> The economic situation is the basis, but the various elements of the super-structure—political forms of the class struggle and its results, to wit: constitutions established by victorious class after a successful battle, etc., juridical forms, and even the reflexes of all these actual struggles in the brains of the participants, political, juristic, philosophical theories, religious views, and their further development into systems of dogmas—also exercise their influence upon the course of the historical struggles and in many cases preponderate in determining their *form*. There is an interaction of all these elements in which, amidst all the endless host of accidents (that is, of things and events whose inner inter-connection is so remote or so impossible of proof that we can regard it as non-existent, as negligible), the economic movement finally asserts itself as necessary. Otherwise the application of the theory to any period of history would be easier than the solution of a simple equation of the first degree.[20]

> The further the particular sphere which we are investigating is removed from the economic sphere and approaches that of pure abstract ideology, the more shall we find it exhibiting accidents in its development, the more will its curve run zigzag. But if you plot the average axis of the curve you will find that this axis will run more and more nearly parallel to the axis of economic development the longer the period considered and the wider the field dealt with.[21]

5. Two Tendencies in the History of Marxism

Throughout the history of Marxism the tendency toward further *schematization* of the course of history has conflicted and alternated with creative effort in the footsteps of Marx's and Engels' *investigation* of history. Yet despite the long-standing official predominance of economism and dogmatism, Marxism has never lost itself irretrievably to schematicism. Like an underground river of great power, it has periodically broken out onto the surface, as witnessed by a constellation of fruitful Marxists whose names today are well known.

In the struggle between schematicizing and investigatory tendencies of Marxism, the first has always fared worse intellectually. The analyses of critical Marxists and Marxologists have repeatedly shown that there is no strict parallelism in the development of the forces of production and the relations of production, not to mention total congruity between the mode of the production of material goods and the social superstructure. There are significant dimensions and moments of social life which are in no way consequences of economic activity. It is not true that the state of all other forms of human activity can be deduced from the state of the activity of material production. The great difficulties that are involved whenever one attempts to distinguish *precisely* the "economic base" from the "social superstructure" are also well known. Thus the Marxologist John Plamenatz (in his *German Marxism and Russian Communism* [1954]), among others, has shown that certain elements of the "social superstructure" simultaneously represent component parts of that very "base" as well.

The belief that there exist "natural laws" of social development which act with "iron necessity" has also turned out to be an illusion. In a word, it is not correct to say that the only thing that remains for people to do is merely to accelerate or slow down the course of history, whose direction and outcome are defined independently of their consciousness, intentions, and will.

Marxists who are unable to escape from schematic frameworks are condemned to deal with pseudo-problems. A typical example is the enormous waste of energy on the question of how it is possible that individual stages are skipped over in the course of social development. It is characteristic of the dogmatic approach first to wed itself to a particular scheme and then to be astonished when development takes an unexpected turn. History, of course, cannot skip over itself, only over schematic thinkers.

For some Marxists it is an unsolved riddle to this day that the socialist revolutions took place in undeveloped countries rather than in developed ones. Instead of questioning their original scheme, they have been more content with the "explanation" according to which this circumstance is the result of a "concurrence of events." Thus the status of "lawfulness" (even "natural," no less) is tacitly maintained for that which has nowhere taken place (socialist revolution as the result of the contradictions of highly developed capitalism), while the rank of "chance" is reserved for that which has already occurred.

In this context it is worth recalling the following explanation of the absence of socialist revolution in the developed capitalist countries: imperialism, extracting superprofits from colonies and in general from dependent countries, enables itself to pacify the working class by creating a "labor aristocracy" and corrupting its leaders. But in the first place, in mature capitalism this stratum undergoes enormous expansion, raising very early on the question of whether it or the constantly dwindling sector of the working class that remains is that class's true representative in these countries. And secondly, assuming that the foregoing argument is at all convincing, the fact remains that it does not conform in the slightest with the economistic scheme. Lenin was one of those Marxists who sought a solution in the manner described above. However bold and original he was, with Trotsky, in theoretically revealing the theoretical possibility of socialist revolution in undeveloped Russia, Lenin was nevertheless unconvincing in resorting to the above palliative.

Schematic thinkers are *always* compelled to deduce the political position of social groups and classes from their economic position. I have already noted that the economistic scheme arose in the course of Marx's study of Western societies and that his analysis of the "Asiatic" mode of production revealed a different theoretical possibility. But regardless, it is no longer possible to view politics from an economistic standpoint. Only if this approach is abandoned is it possible, for example, to understand the genesis of power in the socialist revolutions. For it is a historical fact that in these cases the state-party apparatus achieved economic dominance only after its political dominance had been well established.

6. A Proposed Revision

Into their initial formula concerning the relationship between the forces of production and the relations of production, and between the economic base and the social superstructure, Marx and Engels introduced a series of retrospective modifications, amendments, and clarifications. What in this abundance can be termed an improvement? Generally speaking, those formulations by virtue of which the burden of deterministic dependence and primacy is reduced. This outcome was reached in three senses. First, the causal conceptual apparatus discussed above yielded to a functional one. Next, "reciprocal effects" were increasingly cited, and even "mutual conditioning." Finally, there was a considerable expansion of the temporal and spatial segment of history to which the scheme related, so that the notion of determinism "in the last instance" assumed precedence.

It is impossible to ignore Engels' contribution to these modifications, much as many critics would have us neglect them. Engels, to be sure, was more of a hindrance than a help in many of his interventions. Thus, for instance, the two passages that follow return us to an obviously untenable causal interpretation:

> And if this man has not yet discovered that while the material mode of existence is the *primum agens* this does not preclude the ideological spheres from *reacting upon it in their turn, though with a secondary effect,* he cannot possibly have understood the subject he is writing about.[22]

> These gentlemen often almost deliberately forget that *once a historical element has been brought into the world by other, ultimately economic causes,* it reacts, can react on its environment and even on the causes that have given rise to it.[23]

Nor can the following lines be numbered among Engels' more fortunate pronouncements:

Just as Darwin discovered the law of development of organic nature, so Marx discovered the law of development of human history: *the simple fact, hitherto concealed by an overgrowth of ideology,* that mankind must first of all eat, drink, have shelter and clothing, before it can pursue politics, science, art, religion, etc.; that *therefore* the production of the immediate material means of subsistence and consequently the degree of economic development attained by a given people or during a given epoch form the foundation upon which the state institutions, the legal conceptions, art, and even the ideas on religion, of the people concerned have been evolved, and *in the light of which they must, therefore, be explained,* instead of vice-versa, as had hitherto been the case.[24]

However Engels commits two errors which have long since been noted. Marx quite certainly did not discover that "mankind must first of all eat . . . before it can pursue politics. . . ." This is a trivial fact from time immemorial. From this fact it does not logically follow to reach the conclusion — otherwise much more powerful and non-trivial — that all other human activities must be explained by taking the economic base as the point of departure. It appears that in this passage Engels fails to distinguish between two senses of the "economic base." In the first, the economic base is the absolutely necessary presupposition of existence, and accordingly for any human activity at all. But who has ever questioned that? In the second sense, the state of all other modes of human activity is always derived from the state of economic relations — but this *does not follow* from the first sense of the term and merely remains to be proved.

The same line of reasoning is to be found in Engels' article of 1878, "Karl Marx." To the astonishment of the reader well versed in Marxist theory, Engels here goes so far as to assert that the social superstructure is "quite simply" explained with the assistance of the economic base!

It is self-evident that the future development of the Marxist position must rely on the best versions of Marxism rather than on the most hopeless ones. My revisionist proposal to contribute to this process will exploit and radicalize one of Marx's pronouncements which he expressed in the following words:

Men never relinquish what they have won, but this does not mean that they never relinquish the social form in which they have acquired certain productive forces. On the contrary, *in order that they may not be deprived of the result attained and forfeit the fruits of civilisation, they are obliged, from the moment when their mode of carrying on commerce no longer corresponds to the productive forces acquired, to change all their traditional social forms.*[25]

It is interesting to compare these lines with those that almost immediately precede them:

What is society, whatever its form may be? The product of men's reciprocal action. Are men free to choose this or that form of society? By no means.

Assume a particular state of development in the productive faculties of man and you will get a particular form of commerce and consumption. Assume particular stages of development in production, commerce and consumption and you will have a corresponding social constitution, a corresponding development of the family, of orders or of classes, in a word, a corresponding civil society. Assume a particular civil society and you will get particular political conditions which are only the official expression of civil society.[26]

It is apparent that in the same letter, Marx expounded two different propositions and that he failed to take note of this fact. While the latter is positive and categorical, the former is negative, hypothetical, and teleological—and worthy of our trust.

I would propose the following formulation. *In previous history human societies have had a tendency to pursue changes in the other components (political, legal, religious, etc.) of their lives rather than making the development of material production impossible.* And the relationship between the main components of material production should be described as follows: *in previous history human societies have had a tendency to pursue changes in the relations of production rather than making the development of the forces of production impossible.*

This can also be formulated in an explicitly hypothetical and teleological manner: *in order not to* stagnate, regress, and collapse, human societies *have had to* adapt the relations of production to the development of the forces of production and to adapt all other components of their lives to the needs of the development of material production. In some societies and even civilizations, admittedly, opposite tendencies have indeed dominated, but those societies have therefore stagnated, regressed, and collapsed, often under the blows of more adaptable neighbors and enemies.

At this point we wonder in astonishment how Marx and Engels could have spoken of the "naturalness" of the course of socio-historical development and simultaneously of the *exclusively* (albeit only "in the last instance") deterministic dominance of the economic base. For is not the *helplessness* of individual societies and civilizations to remove their own obstacles to the development of material production also one of the manifestations of that very "naturalness" (=spontaneity)?

It is important to stress that the outcome of the conflict under discussion here depends upon human needs, desires, interests, knowledge, abilities, and power taken collectively. It is in this way that the reification of history, and an understanding of history as some kind of subject and actor, can be avoided. Whether the members of a society are capable of identifying barriers to the development of material production—and if so whether they possess in sufficient degree not only the need, desire, and interest but also the knowledge, abilities, and powers to eliminate them—is of crucial significance. Marx and Engels, to be sure, knew that people with their knowledge, abilities, and powers represent a productive force, even the most decisive one. But my point here involves knowledge, abilities, and powers *of another order,* without which neither productive knowledge, nor ability, nor power can prevail. In this respect, too, nothing happens automatically or even smoothly, but rather in conflict (including class conflict) and with setbacks. What is more, the latter order of willing dispositions are incomparably less cumulative than the former.

Undoubtedly, Marx and Engels were aware of cases of immobilism and regression in the course of history. But why did they never draw a sufficiently radical revisionist conclusion from this regarding their generalization about the dominance of the economic base? That generalization is well grounded in history once, and to the extent that, it assumes a global rather than a local character. The further we go into the past, the less Marx and Engels are right. And vice-versa: their generalizations become increasingly accurate the more interdependent human societies have become and the more that global expectations and standards have developed under mutual influence and pressure. Nor were they able to overcome adequately the temptation of the investigator and theorist of history to make generalizations using successful, adaptable, and victorious societies as the point of departure. It is time that Marxism took greater account than it has before of the victims of historical selection.

7. Classical Marxism on the Role of Famous Personalities

Marx did little to clarify his position on the place of exceptional individuals in the socio-historical process. One of his rare *general* statements on this topic reads as follows:

> World history would indeed be very easy to make, if the struggle were taken upon only on condition of infallibly favourable chances. It would, on the other hand, be of a very mystical nature if 'accidents' played no part. *These accidents themselves fall naturally into the general course of development and are compensated again by other accidents. But acceleration and delay are very dependent upon such 'accidents,' which include the 'accident' of the character of those who at first stand at the head of the movement.*[27]

Thus according to Marx there is a "general course of development," and giants can only contribute to its acceleration or delay but not change it in any way. Engels makes this determinism even more severe:

> That such and such a man and precisely that man arises at a particular time in a particular country is, of course, pure chance. *But cut him out and there will be a demand for a substitute, and this substitute will be found, good or bad, but in the long run he will be found.* That Napoleon, just that particular Corsican, should have been the military dictator whom the French Republic,

exhausted by it own warfare, had rendered necessary, was chance, but that, if a Napoleon had been lacking, another would have filled the place, is proved by the fact that *the man was always found as soon as he became necessary:* Caesar, Augustus, Cromwell, etc. While Marx discovered the materialist conception of history, Thierry, Mignet, Guizot, and all the English historians up to 1850 are evidence that it was being striven for, and the discovery of the same conception by Morgan proves that the time was ripe for it and that it simply *had* to be discovered.[28]

In the phrase "good or bad" Engels neglects the essential difference between good and bad substitutes. Moreover it begs the question of how to verify Engels' assertion at all when there have been no substitutes. His reductionistic-deterministic exaggeration cannot be justified even if one takes into account the real need that existed at the time of opposing the idea of history as the creation of great men.

The fate of Engels' work is itself the most persuasive refutation of his notion of substitutability. It was as if his followers competed amongst themselves in extrapolating the most minute threads of his opus. Thus the above idea, with Plekhanov, grew into an entire book, which was as influential as it was bad. I quote:

> Approximately the same thing may be said about Robespierre. Let us assume that he was an absolutely indispensable force in his party; but even so, he was not the only force. If the accidental fall of a brick had killed him, say, in January, 1793, *his place would, of course, have been taken by somebody else, and although this person might have been inferior to him in every respect, nevertheless, events would have taken the same course as they did when Robespierre was alive.*[29]

This is utterly improbable. If the place of one historical personality is taken by another who is "in every respect" inferior, this would not have any impact even on the *course of events!* No, this was no mere slip on Plekhanov's part:

> Let us assume that the other general who had secured this place would have been more peaceful than Napoleon, that he would not have roused the whole of Europe against himself, and therefore, would have died in the Tuileries and not on the island of St. Helens. In that case, the Bourbons would not have returned to France at all; for them, such a result would certainly have been the "opposite" of what it was. In its relation to the internal life of France as a whole, however, this result would have differed little from the actual result. . . All such changes in the course of events might, to some extent, have influenced the subsequent political, and through it, the economic life of Europe. Nevertheless, under no circumstances would the final outcome of the revolutionary movement have been the "opposite" of what it was. Owing to the specific qualities of their minds and characters, influential individuals can change

the *individual features of events and some of their particular consequences,* but they cannot change their general *trend,* which is determined by other forces.[30]

I hope I may be forgiven if I reproduce in its entirety Sartre's commentary, before which, with no exaggeration, Plekhanov's position falls to pieces:

This passage, which has always made me laugh, I quote from the old-fashioned Plekhanov because I do not believe that Marxists have made any progress in this respect. There is no doubt that the final outcome would not have been different from what it was. But let us look at the variables which are eliminated: the bloody Napoleonic battles, the influence of revolutionary ideology on Europe, the occupation of France by the Allies, the return of the landowners, and the white Terror. Economically, as has been established today, the Restoration was a period of regression for France; the conflict between the property owners and the new bourgeoisie of the Empire delayed the development of the sciences and industry; the economic revival dates from 1830. One may admit that the advance of the bourgeoisie under a more peaceful emperor would not have been arrested and that France would not have kept that flavor of the *"Ancien Régime"* which so strongly impressed English visitors. As for the liberal movement, if it had come about at all, it would not have resembled the movement of 1830 in any way, since it would have lacked precisely the economic basis. Apart from all *that,* of course, the evolution would have been the same. Only, the "that," which is so disdainfully tossed over to the ranks of chance, is the whole life of men. Plekhanov, undismayed, looks on the terrible bloodshed of the Napoleonic wars, from which France was such a long time in recovering; he remains indifferent to the slowing up of economic and social life which marks the return of the Bourbons and from which the whole population had to suffer; he neglects the widespread misery which at about 1815 provoked the bourgeoisie into combat with religious fanaticism. As for the men who lived, suffered, and struggled under the Restoration and who ultimately got rid of the throne, no one of them would have been what he was or would have existed as such if Napoleon had not accomplished his *coup d'état.* What becomes of Hugo if his father is not a general of the Empire? And Musset? And Flaubert, who, as we have indicated, internalized the conflict between skepticism and faith? If after this we are told that these changes cannot modify the development of productive forces and the relations of production in the course of the last century, this is a truism. But if this development is to be made the sole object of human history, we simply fall back into the "economism" which we wanted to avoid; and Marxism becomes an "inhumanism."[31]

8. The Lenin/Trotsky Turning Point

Lenin and Trotsky effected a sharp turn from economistic-naturalistic determinism to the decisive role of organized revolutionary actors. This activist break was so great that at times it bordered on voluntarism and even crossed over into it. Yet at one level their work is permeated by general assertions about society and history by means of which the economistic and naturalistic positions are reaffirmed *without restriction.* Thus Lenin wrote in his "What the 'Friends of the People' Are and How They Fight the Social-Democrats" (and made the same assessment many years later in his article on Karl Marx):

This idea of materialism in sociology was in itself a stroke of genius. Naturally, *for the time being* it was only a hypothesis, but one which first created the possibility of a strictly scientific approach to historical and social problems. . . . Materialism removed this contradiction by carrying the analysis deeper, to the origin of man's social ideas themselves; and its conclusion that the course of ideas depends on the course of things is the only one compatible with scientific psychology. Further, and from yet another aspect, this hypothesis was the first to elevate sociology to the level of a science. . . . Thirdly, and finally, another reason why this hypothesis for the first time made a *scientific* sociology possible was that *only* the reduction of social relations to production relations and of the latter to the level of the productive forces, provided a firm basis for the conception that the development of formations of society is *a process of natural history.* And it goes without saying that without such a view there can be no social science. (The subjectivists, for instance, although they admitted that historical phenomena conform to law, were incapable of regarding their evolution as a process of natural history, precisely because they came to a halt before man's social ideas and aims and *were unable to reduce them to material* social relations.[32]

But when *concrete* phenomena and events had to be explained, and even more when they employed theory as a direct instrument of revolutionary action, both Lenin and Trotsky almost totally freed themselves from their economistic-naturalistic fetters.

Indeed, in speaking of Russia, even Marx himself on occasion deviated from his economistic-naturalistic determinism. Thus in his 1881 letter to Vera Zasulich he asserted that the Russian village communes did not need to fall victim to capitalist development. And in his Preface to the Russian edition of *The Communist Manifesto* in 1882 he allowed the possibility that they might develop into a higher, communist form of land tenure. Finally, in a letter written in 1877 but published in Russia only after his death, Marx responded to the criticism of Mikhailovsky, who had abandoned the notion that Russia must not pass through a capitalist period. Parenthetically, Marx's counterattack on Mikhailovsky contained an inaccuracy, for it was not correct to say that Mikhailovsky groundlessly attributed to him the aspiration of formulating a general theory of historical development valid for all previous societies.

To be sure, Marx and Engels clung to the end to their belief that the eventual socialist revolution in Russia would survive only if it were followed by revolution in Western Europe. This condition was to be used by Trotsky in his effort to establish a bridge, however flimsy, between his vision of permanent revolution and classical Marxism.

The creative confrontation of Lenin and Trotsky with the needs of revolutionary practice resulted in two epochal innovations in the history of Marxism. In opposing the Western Social Democrats and the domestic Mensheviks, Lenin shifted the emphasis from the economic and other objective preconditions to a centralized organization of professional revolutionaries as the motive force and vanguard of the coming revolution. In a questionnaire circulated a few years ago, important figures in Western social science included this discovery by Lenin as one of the most significant and influential of this century. While I agree, I do not wish to lose sight of the fact that Lenin's views on revolutionary organization had their origins in Tkachev, and even earlier in Blanqui.

With his concept of the revolutionary party, Lenin made a sizeable activist breach in the economistic-deterministic floodgates. But that shift was not in itself sufficient to prepare the theoretical transition to socialist revolution. Only in conjunction with Trotsky's idea of permanent revolution (borrowed in part from Parvus, and to a certain extent from Marx) did Lenin reveal the possibility in Marxism for socialist revolution in backward Russia. The young Gramsci would later call this "the revolution against *Capital.*" It would, however, be more accurate if we were to characterize it, along with the other socialist revolutions, as a *revolution against economistic-naturalistic determinism.*

At first Trotsky decisively rejected Lenin's ideas concerning the organization of the revolutionary party. In *Our Political Tasks* (1904), he severely reproached Lenin for the Jacobin conception of organization which the latter had developed in *What Is to Be Done?* (1902), and made this warning and prediction: "Lenin's methods lead to this: the party organization at first substitutes itself for the Party as a whole; then the Central Committee substitutes itself for the organization; and finally a single 'dictator' substitutes himself for the Central Committee."

Did Lenin, in dictating his "Testament" and the subsequent "Postscript,"* remember Trotsky's warning? The question is appropriate, regardless of the fact that in the meantime Trotsky himself had contributed in a substantial way to the establishment of relationships in the Party that had created the possibility of moving in the direction he had described in 1904.

On what did Lenin focus his anxieties, sensing that his end was near? On the personal qualities of the leaders of the Bolshevik Party and the Revolution— Stalin, Trotsky, Zinoviev, Kamenev, Bukharin, and Piatakov. He feared a split in the Party because of conflicts, as he wrote, between the two most

---

*The author refers to documents written by Lenin on December 23 and 25, 1922 and January 4, 1923 respectively, shortly before his death.

important members of the Central Committee, Stalin and Trotsky. Having become General Secretary, Stalin had concentrated enormous power in his hands, and the question, wrote Lenin with a foreboding of things to come, was whether he knew how to use it with sufficient caution. Of Trotsky, Lenin wrote that he was the most capable member of the Central Committee, but that he was excessively self-assured and inclined to seek administrative solutions to problems.

In the Postscript Lenin continued with his psychological analysis. He came to the conclusion that Stalin was too rude, a quality that becomes extremely dangerous for someone in his position. Therefore Lenin proposed that he be replaced by someone more tolerant, more loyal, more polite, and more considerate toward his comrades—in a word, someone less capricious. At first glance these were trifles, but, according to Lenin, of such a nature that they could assume "decisive significance."

Did not all this constitute a *practical* acknowledgment that Trotsky had been right in 1904? For our argument it is more important, however, that Lenin's insight that personal qualities and conflicts can achieve "decisive significance" has nothing in common with economistic-naturalistic determinism, according to which the most prominent individuals are nevertheless replaceable factors and expressions of the inevitable course of history. This impression of inconsistency on Lenin's part remains even when it is taken into account that Lenin also sought an *institutional* solution to the above situation—in protecting the union of the workers and the peasantry, in the strengthening of the Workers' Inspection, and in increasing the size of the Central Committee membership.

It is characteristic that the introduction of these changes into Marxism required a thinker who, through his *personal experience,* could see how enormous political and other types of power could accumulate in the hands of the leadership. This experience was lacking to both Marx and Engels as well as to Plekhanov, from all of whom Lenin indeed learned, at an abstract theoretical level, to reduce the role of the most significant personalities to an absolute minimum.

Trotsky reflected and wrote about the role of historical giants much more extensively than Lenin. In this context it is important to remember that he often repeated his judgment that the Bolshevik Revolution would never have occurred had it not been for Lenin. Trotsky ascribed a similar place in later events to Stalin—with a reverse, negative sign, to be sure. How far such judgments bring us from economistic and naturalistic determinism!

9. Introductory Remarks on the Problem of Charisma in Marxism

It must be acknowledged that the conceptual linkage between economistic-naturalistic determinism and Lenin's statements concerning the potentially "decisive significance" of the leader was being strained to the breaking point. Shortly after his death it was to snap under the impact of the allegedly Marxist construction of the new society and the apologia for Stalin's supercult. The "expanded reproduction" (Lukács) of that cult was accompanied by the continued propagation of an explicitly deterministic doctrine in the form of "historical materialism." At the same time, those who merely hinted at the idea of the substitutability of the leader were made to pay with their heads.

Later, Khrushchev's unquestionably progressive critique of the "cult of personality" was nonetheless no more Marxist in content. Stalin was merely redesignated from the source of all that was good to the role of the demiurge of all that was evil.

How is it that communist parties, which *in theory* invoke so persistently the deterministic formula with the "natural laws" and "iron necessity" of the course of history, so often have such a vital dependence *in practice* on their own leadership? There have been few movements in history whose theory has so diminished the role of the greatest individuals in favor of collective actors and impersonal social forces, and in which the role of the leading personalities at crucial junctures has been so fateful.

Of such theories it could not be expected that they would be a source of inspiration for the introduction of effective controls on the behavior of leaders. Instead of being conscious and free creators of history, communist party members have often become adherents, followers, and partisans of their own charismatic chieftans, and at times simply dictators.

Thus, in the midst of a movement which invokes Marxism day in and day out, the thesis of great personalities as replaceable contingencies in the framework of the inevitable course of history has been refuted in practice. This thesis is all the more untenable in the modern world, in which the power in the hands of statesmen is so great that they are capable of making decisions which literally affect the existence, or the destruction, of humanity as a whole.

None of this, of course, is to advocate a return to the approach which seeks to locate the mainspring of history in the idiosyncracies of the leader. Nothing can be said *a priori* concerning these idiosyncracies, for whether leaders play a decisive or more or less negligible role is a matter which depends in turn upon the nature of concrete societies, tradition, the structure of groups and institutions, as well as the force of circumstance. To give a concrete example, it is certain that Stalin would not have arrogated so much power had he not relied upon the power and charisma of the centralized Bolshevik Party and, even more importantly, its apparatus.

At this point some conceptual clarification is in order. The reader has most likely become accustomed to associating the concept of charisma exclusively with personality, as in Weber's classical definition:

> The term 'charisma' will be applied to a certain quality of an individual personality by virtue of which he is set apart from ordinary men and treated as

endowed with supernatural, superhuman, or at least specifically exceptional powers or qualities. These are such as are not accessible to the ordinary person, but are regarded as of divine origin or as exemplary, and on the basis of them the individual concerned is treated as a leader.[33]

In the more recent literature, however, the meaning of the term "charisma" has quite visibly been broadened. The prominent sociologist Edward Shils has gone the farthest in this direction:

> In all societies deference is accorded to authoritative roles, their incumbents, and the norms they promulgate in consideration of their capacity to create, maintain, and change the order of society. In all societies there is a propensity in most human beings, on occasion, to perceive, beyond immediate and particular events, the forces, principles, and powers which govern the immediate and the particular and which impose and necessitate an order which embraces them. Particularly serious attention and respect are given to what are thought to be those transcendent powers which are manifested in the orders of nature and society and in patterns of norms which intend the ordering of human action. Where institutions, roles, persons, norms, or symbols are perceived or believed to be connected or infused with these transcendent powers, we say they are perceived to be charismatic.
>
> *Charisma, then, is the quality which is imputed to persons, actions, roles, institutions, symbols, and material objects* because of their presumed connection with "ultimate," "fundamental," "vital," order-determining powers.[34]

In Shils' definition, unfortunately, there is unclear connotation and overly broad denotation. What we really need is a concept which would embrace both *individuals* and *collectives* (individual and collective charisma), but certainly not non-human entities. This restricted denotational expansion should be introduced into Weber's definition cited above: collective charisma is usually "intensive" and "concentrated" (Shils' expressions) personification, although there are cases in which individual charisma dries up while collective charisma survives.

In the theory of Marx and Engels no real basis can be found for the charismatic relationship of the followers toward the leaders of the movement who appeal to them. But what is the situation in this regard concerning the collective charisma of the communist party? The following well-known passage provides the most relevant grounds for a response:

> In what relation do the Communists stand to the proletarians as a whole?
> The Communists do not form a separate party opposed to other working-class parties.
> They have no interests separate and apart from those of the proletariat as a whole.
> They do not set up any sectarian principles of their own, by which to shape and mould the proletarian movement.

The Communists are distinguished from the other working-class parties by this only: (1) In the national struggles of the proletarians of the different countries, they point out and bring to the front the common interests of the entire proletariat, independently of all nationality. (2) In the various stages of development which the struggle of the working class against the bourgeoisie has to pass through, they always and everywhere represent the interests of the movement as a whole.

The Communists, therefore, are on the one hand, practically, the most advanced and resolute section of the working-class parties of every country, that section which pushes forward all others; on the other hand, theoretically, they have over the great mass of the proletariat the advantage of clearly understanding the line of march, the conditions, and the ultimate general results of the proletarian movement. [35]

It would seem, then, that in the minds of Marx and Engels the potential for the "charismatization" of the communist party is relatively weak. In any event, the party as it appeared to them was a far cry from what it would become for its adherents in our time.

NOTES TO PART ONE

1. Ludwig Wittgenstein, *Tractatus logico-philosophicus,* trans. D. F. Pears and B. F. McGuiness (London: Routledge and Paul, 1961), p. 147.
2. Richard J. Bernstein, *Praxis and Action: Contemporary Philosophies of Human Activity* (Philadelphia: University of Pennsylvania Press, 1971), pp. 302–303.
3. Friedrich Engels, "Outline of a Critique of Political Economy," in Karl Marx and Friedrich Engels, *Collected Works,* vol. III (New York: International Publishers, 1975), p. 433.
4. Friedrich Engels, Letter to J. Bloch of September 21–22, 1890, in *Basic Writings on Politics and Philosophy: Karl Marx and Friedrich Engels,* ed. Lewis S. Feuer (Garden City: Doubleday, 1959), p. 399.
5. Karl Marx, *Capital,* "Afterword to the Second German Edition," in *The Marx-Engels Reader* (2nd ed.), ed. Robert C. Tucker (New York: Norton, 1978), p. 300; my emphasis—S.S.
6. Marx, *Capital,* vol. I, in *ibid.,* p. 323; my emphasis—S.S.
7. Marx, *Capital,* "Preface to the First German Edition," in *ibid.,* p. 296; my emphasis—S.S.
8. Karl Marx, *Capital,* vol. III (New York: International Publishers, 1967), p. 178.
9. See Georg Henrik von Wright, *Erklären und Verstehen* (Frankfurt(M.): Athenäum-Verlag, 1974).
10. Marx to L. Kugelmann, Letter of 11 July 1868, in Karl Marx and Friedrich Engels, *Selected Correspondence,* 2nd ed. (Moscow: Progress, 1965), p. 209.
11. Karl Marx, *The Holy Family;* see *Karl Marx: Selected Writings in Sociology and Social Philosophy,* ed. T. B. Bottomore and Maximilien Rubel (New York: McGraw-Hill, 1956), p. 58.
12. *Ibid.,* p. 63.
13. Karl Marx, "The German Ideology," in *The Marx-Engels Reader,* p. 272.
14. Jürgen Habermas, "Thesen zur Rekonstruktion des Historischen Materialismus," Stuttgart Hegelkongress, May 1975; compare with Habermas' *Zur Rekonstruktion des Historischen Materialismus* (Frankfurt(M.): Suhrkamp, 1976), p. 158.
15. Karl Marx, "The Poverty of Philosophy," in *Writings of the Young Marx on Philosophy and*

Society, ed. Lloyd D. Easton and Kurt H. Guddat (Garden City: Doubleday, 1967), p. 480; my emphasis—S.S.

16. *Ibid.,* p. 491; my emphasis—S.S.
17. Karl Marx, "Theories of Surplus Value," in *Karl Marx: Selected Writings in Sociology and Social Philosophy,* p. 100.
18. Friedrich Engels, Letter to J. Bloch of September 21-22, 1890.
19. *Ibid.,* pp. 397-398.
20. *Ibid.,* p. 398.
21. Friedrich Engels, Letter to W. Borgius of 25 January 1894; until recently this was erroneously identified as a letter to H. Starkenberg. [Translator's Note: An English-language source for this letter is in *ibid.,* p. 412.]
22. Friedrich Engels, Letter to C. Schmidt of August 5, 1890, in *ibid.,* p. 396. With the exception of the words *"Primum agens,"* all emphases are mine—S.S.
23. Friedrich Engels, Letter to F. Mehring of July 14, 1893, in *The Marx-Engels Reader,* p. 767; my emphasis—S.S.
24. Friedrich Engels, "Speech at the Graveside of Karl Marx," in *ibid.,* p. 681; my emphasis—S.S.
25. Karl Marx, Letter to P. V. Annenkov of December 28, 1846, in *ibid.,* p. 137; my emphasis—S.S.
26. *Ibid.,* pp. 136-137; my emphasis—S.S.
27. Marx to Kugelmann, *loc. cit.;* my emphasis—S.S.
28. Marx to Borgius, *op. cit.,* pp. 411-412; with the exception of the word "had," all emphases are my own—S.S.
29. G. Plekhanov, "The Role of the Individual in History," in *Essays in Historical Materialism* (New York: International Publishers, 1940), p. 45; with the exception of the words "the same course," all emphases are my own—S.S.
30. *Ibid.,* p. 48.
31. Jean-Paul Sartre, *Search for a Method,* trans. Hazel E. Barnes (New York: Knopf, 1963; Vintage, 1968), pp. 131-132.
32. V. I. Lenin, "What the 'Friends of the People' Are and How They Fight the Social-Democrats," *Collected Works,* vol. I (Moscow: Foreign Language Publishing House, 1963), pp. 139-141.
33. Max Weber, *The Theory of Social and Economic Organization,* trans. A. M. Henderson and Talcott Parsons (New York: Free Press, 1947), pp. 358-359.
34. Edward Shils, "Charisma," in *International Encyclopedia of the Social Sciences,* ed. David L. Sills (New York: Macmillan, 1968), vol. 2, p. 386.
35. Karl Marx and Friedrich Engels, "Manifesto of the Communist Party," in *The Marx-Engels Reader,* pp. 483-484.

Part Two
Authoritarian and Democratic Communism

1. An Archetype: Authoritarian-Pauperistic Communism

Socialism cannot develop so long as there is continued mass *poverty*. The concept of poverty is among the most valuable for the Marxist understanding of history. In this respect it is essential to consider not only material poverty, but also destitution of all kinds. There is also need of introducing the concept of *political poverty*. It is characteristic of this type of poverty that the citizen has no opportunity to exert real influence on the making of fundamental social decisions.

All the socialist revolutions have taken place in societies distinctly marked by material and political poverty. At the same time, these were societies of material and political abundance for the small ruling circles and classes. These circumstances gave rise to *authoritarian-pauperistic communism* as a revolutionary response to social immobility, inequality, injustice, and privilege.

The characteristics of this type of communism are as follows:

1. A centralized revolutionary party that aspires to establish a power monopoly;
2. Violence as an obligatory, and the principal, revolutionary instrumentality;
3. Total subordination of the individual to the collective undertaking;
4. Ascetic self-denial;
5. Leveling in material distribution and life style (*uranilovka,* in Russian).

The first characteristic, strict hierarchical order, defines the framework and the boundaries of the entire whole. The relative weight and importance of the remaining characteristics follow in the order given above.

It should be cautioned that the foregoing is a description only of the "ideal type" of authoritarian-pauperistic communism. This form of communism was predominant in the course of the preparation and conduct of *all* socialist revolutions and in the period immediately following them. The differences among communist parties and revolutions become conspicuous only in the latter period, although subsequently they become enormous. And since their paths and results do differ so extensively, it is obvious that our assessments of them must also be no less varied.

Marx would probably have called this type of communism "primitive" and "despotic."[1] Marx's communism, on the other hand, presupposes a

> great increase in productive power, a high degree of its development. And, on the other hand, this development of productive forces (which itself implies the actual empirical existence of men in their *world-historical,* instead of local, being) is an absolutely necessary practical premise because without it *want* is merely made general, and with *destitution* the struggle for necessities and all the old filthy business would necessarily be reproduced. . . .[2]

In contrast to collectivism (3), asceticism (4), and *uravnilovka* (5) as characteristics of pauperistic communism, Marx's *communism of abundance* is distinguished by solidaristic personalism and associationism, humanistic hedonism, and the principle of distributive justice according to need, for which the way must be paved historically by distribution according to work. No one who is familiar with Marx could deny any of this.

But partly for this reason there are many Marxologists who would maintain that Marx's communism is also authoritarian, albeit not pauperistic. They would undoubtedly find a match with the first two characteristics of authoritarian-pauperistic communism as described above in Marx's definition of the dictatorship of the proletariat and of revolutionary violence as the "midwife" of the new society. I do not dispute that there is a certain amount of overlap here, but an identity is out of the question. For Marx envisioned the dictatorship of the proletariat, but not the dictatorship of the communist party. The dictatorship of the proletariat was to have been a very short-lived dictatorship of the vast majority of the population over the dispossessed minority. Marx did not imagine the communist party as the sole proletarian party. The absolutization of revolutionary violence was also far from his mind. And in several of the most developed capitalist countries[3] he acknowledged the possibility of a nonviolent transition to socialism, which is not the case with that variant of communism which finds its prototype in Leninism.[4]

Instead of preserving their capacity for critical understanding and evaluation, many Marxists have totally identified with the socialist revolutions, linking their utopian hopes to them. Bitter disappointment has been the inevitable result. There are some who have still not learned their lesson, moving their utopia from one country to another: from the USSR to China, from there to Cuba. . . .

The opposite extreme threatens those who would detach authoritarian-pauperistic communism from concrete socio-historical circumstances altogether and, abstracted from reality, compare it with Marx's vision. In this event Marx becomes completely irrelevant to an understanding of the social revolutions of the twentieth century, while his utopia of abundance could even serve counter-revolutionary goals.

In this case Marx would suffer a fate similar to that of liberalism:

> To the world's range of enormous problems, liberalism responds with its verbal fetish of "Freedom" plus a shifting series of opportunistic reactions. The world is hungry; the liberal cries, "Let us make it free!" The world is tired of war; the liberal cries, "Let us arm for peace!" The peoples of the world are without land; the liberal cries, "Let us beg the landed oligarchs to parcel some of it out!" In sum: the most grievous charge today against liberalism and its conservative varieties is that they are so utterly *provincial,* and thus so irrelevant to the major problems that must now be confronted in so many areas of the world.[5]

Contemporary liberalism, for the most part, has no conception of social change applicable to economically undeveloped countries ruled by dictatorships. As if the classics of liberalism did not acknowledge the right of the people to violent revolution! Violence and the dictatorship of revolutionaries are the weak points of modern liberalism and Marxism alike, each in its own way. The liberal prejudice against revolutionary violence and dictatorship, even when all hope has vanished that necessary social changes will be carried out peacefully, is obstinate indeed. This is what happens when one's very own tradition, both historical and theoretical, is abandoned to collective oblivion.

Marxists have hitherto been powerless to find practical answers to the following two questions: how to diminish authoritarianism and centralism in a revolutionary organization that has been driven underground and obliged to apply force? and how to democratize a revolutionary dictatorship once it has been established?

Circumstances of economic and political poverty provide nearly irresistably favorable conditions for the violent and authoritarian revolutionary organization. Practically as if by law, communist-led revolutions have been victorious in conditions of dictatorship, war, and foreign occupation. All this is fine, the liberal will retort, but socialist revolutions have failed to establish the freedoms of association, striking, peaceful demonstration, travel, expression, scientific and philosophical research, artistic creativity. . . . True, counters the communist, but they have made possible agrarian reform, industrialization, the elimination of mass starvation, of illiteracy, epidemics, the distribution of national wealth to the advantage of the upper strata and classes—and this, too, is undoubtedly of humanistic import.

To be sure, communists of the Stalinist ilk have adopted the practice of simply contrasting the facts about human suffering to proofs of *economic and cultural progress* achieved under their leadership. As if these were values of the same order! In assessing the total impact of each of the socialist revolutions, the *decisive* factor is that of the *human cost* (the "pyramids of sacrifice"[6]) at which such progress has been achieved—and it unquestionably varies widely from case to case.

The basic contradiction of this variety of communism consists in the struggle for the *emancipation* of man through explicitly *authoritarian* means. The choice of such means is largely defined by the nature of the regime against which the communist revolutionaries in question have arisen. There is much truth in Sartre's comment that "one must become what one's opponent is in order to struggle successfully against him."[7] The other components of the authoritarian social milieu in which this type of communism arises also leave their mark, from education in the family and in school, through management in the factory and in general at the work place, to the dominant political culture itself.

In the midst of impoverishment and dictatorship, no one is capable of being a revolutionary unless he is prepared for collective zeal, denial, and egalitarianism. In the literature on communism we often come across the concept of the egalitarian syndrome. This is often linked with the superficial and fundamentally erroneous assertion that the aforementioned absolutization of equality has led to unfreedom. In fact this collectivistic and ascetic egalitarianism was partial and fragile from the start, for it was put into practice under conditions of political superordination and subordination. It was surely to be expected that sooner or later some politically powerful figures would attempt to create material privileges for themselves. Stalin's critique of *uravnilovka* was adopted as an axiom in other communist parties as well. Individual professional revolutionaries must have regarded an extravagant life style as a necessity in order to camouflage themselves from their persecutors. When they in turn become the wielders of power, of course, this rationale evaporated, but the old habits remained.

Any comparison between pauperistic communism and Marx's communism of abundance should take into account the fact that Marx belonged to the optimistic tradition which assumed the possibility of unlimited economic growth. But of late it has become an ever more commonly shared conviction that economic development will ultimately be restricted or even totally halted as a result of the exhaustion of raw materials and energy, environmental pollution, and a host of other factors. Eminent scientists and scholars speak of "spaceship earth" or anticipate a "stationary equilibrium."[8] We will, it is claimed, have to reduce investments in economic development in order to give future generations a chance. On the other hand, there are many who counter this pessimism with prospects for the exploitation of new types of energy, technological innovation, birth control, changing consumer attitudes, and the like.

It is astonishing that Marxists, for whom the relationship of man to nature is the key to understanding the movement of history, have not yet seriously joined in this debate. To be sure, with his thesis of "communism without growth" the East German thinker Wolfgang Harich[9] has issued a challenge to all Marxists. Instead of the withering away of the state into a society of material superabundance, he foresees a powerful communist state which will effectuate an ascetic mode of distribution and maintain economic equilibrium without growth—all this in the interest of preserving the biosphere.

Other Marxists, of course, need not be inclined to Harich's pessimism, but for this reason they must join in a re-examination of the vision of material abundance. After all, the irrational growth of consumer appetites in the West is often projected into that vision. It is also abused in terms of postponing democratization even in those communist countries that are economically developed. But how much longer must we wait for socialist democracy? Bourgeois democracy was born at a lower level of economic development.

2. The Humanization of Violent Revolution

The twentieth century has been characterized by world wars and revolutions. Explosions of revolutionary violence have most commonly burst forth in times of war.

While historians, sociologists, and political scientists have devoted much study to the revolutions of the twentieth century, ethical theorists have done so only as an exception. Under the sway of neopositivism, the bulk of academic ethics until recently has steered clear of socio-political themes. Analytical philosophy, narrowed to questions of meta-ethics, was totally constrained to abstain from the normative approach. Fortunately, philosophers of other orientations—phenomenological, existential, Marxist, personalist—were not led astray. We owe some of them a debt of gratitude for their significant contributions on the relationship between revolution and morality.

Mass violence is characterized by marginal situations in which because of the conflict of fundamental moral principles, no very reliable and precise guideposts are available. Nowhere does the clash of the teleological and deontological positions manifest itself more forcefully than in circumstances of revolution and war.

In collective undertakings such as revolutions, all moral problems are made enormously complex. An ethics which proceeds from everyday individual relationships is totally inappropriate in considerations of revolutionary activity.

In order to indicate the difficulties with which an ethics of revolution must contend, let us take the problem of the responsibility of the revolutionary. How are we to define the individual's share in the collective result? What real opportunities for choice are open to the individual in the context of disciplined collective action? Can the consequences of revolutionary undertakings be foreseen, and if so to what extent? How are we to define the revolutionary's responsibility when there is already a difference, and even a contradiction, between his intentions and expectations and the results of his actions?

The moral problems of revolution attracted little concern among Bolshevik leaders. In the *ABC of Communism* by Bukharin and Preobrazhensky, these questions are totally absent. Exceptions were made only when it became necessary to defend the revolution on ethical grounds. It was in this spirit that Lenin and Trotsky attacked Kautsky on a number of occasions. Almost twenty years later Trotsky once again took up the same theme in his essays "Their Morals and Ours" and "Moralists and Sycophants Against Marxism." The former was occasioned by a critique by John Dewey entitled "Means and Ends." Trotsky did not respond to it directly, for the characteristic reason that he did not have a good answer.

Indeed at times Trotsky rejected the very question of the justification of revolution, as when he wrote: "Do the consequences of a revolution justify in general the sacrifices it involves? . . . It would be as well to ask in face of the difficulties and griefs of personal existence: Is it worth while to be born?"[10] By drawing this comparison Trotsky wants to make the question of the justification of revolution *senseless* instead of showing that revolution is justified only in the sense of being *inevitable.* The latter kind of deterministic error, we are to conclude, might only have been committed by a less cultivated revolutionary. Yet the above analogy with a natural occurrence might have been supportable had the October Revolution been a spontaneous event. It is an historical fact, however, that this revolution was organizationally directed.

By the manner in which they approached the task of justifying their own revolution, the Bolshevik leaders established a model for communist revolutionaries in other countries. Unfortunately, the Bolsheviks attempted to defend nearly *every* revolutionary measure on moral grounds instead of defending the revolution in *summary* form. It is true that these were reactions to attacks which exhibited not the slightest appreciation of the situation in which the Bolsheviks resorted to violence. If the issue is one of victims and responsibility, then we must not lose sight of the Tsarist autocracy, mass poverty and starvation, the nonexistence of health services for broad strata of the population, and the millions of dead and crippled during the First World War (from which the Bolsheviks extracted Russia). And as concerns terror, the fact is that the Bolsheviks used it in self-defense against the terror of the "Whites" and foreign interventionists. Moreover, in the seizure of power of October 1917 exceptionally little violence was employed.

The dictatorship of the proletariat, according to Lenin, just like any other dictatorship, represents "rule based directly upon force and unrestricted by any laws."[11] This understanding of the matter, to put it mildly, did little to contribute to the humanization of the revolution. Revolutions are bound by no legal norms, nor certainly were the Bolsheviks themselves bound by religious-humanistic norms. Only moral considerations, then, remained. And once they, too, are rejected, everything is abandoned (solely) to the will of the revolutionary.

It is incumbent on the revolutionary not to do all that is in his power. Marxist ethics must render this relationship between "can" and "ought" in revolutionary activity more precise. Once the influence of Stalinism became predominant, many communists lived in fear of not being radical enough instead of attempting to act humanely. For the Stalinists, radicalism meant that one must persecute and kill as many people as possible in order to "nip in the bud" undesirable phenomena with the "sword of the revolution."

Since violence always tends to beget violence, the revolutionary's main concern must be to reduce violence and to humanize it, and not to overcome "prejudices" against its use. It is symptomatic that it is a rare revolutionary *leader* who is *himself* prepared to kill. Why should not revolution, as well as "rebellion" (Camus), be capable of defining humanistic boundaries which ought not to be crossed? A crime in the name of revolution is just as much a crime as that committed in the name of counterrevolution. The Marxist revolutionary must declare himself for socialism or for barbarism. Violence, in the best case, will serve to eliminate certain obstacles, but violence will not create a humane society.

While it is very difficult to control mass hatred and the craving for vengeance, those who do not invest the maximum of effort in this task have no right to call themselves a Marxist vanguard. No matter how sincerely its goal may be the creation of a new world and the beginning of true "history," revolutionary violence itself belongs to the old world and "prehistory."

From the judgment that a revolution is justified, it does not follow that all levels of violence in it are also justified. There is also an essential difference between those revolutionaries who are conscious that they often must choose between a greater and a lesser evil and those who always believe themselves to opt for good against evil. Thanks to the latter, socialist revolutions have produced a great *surplus of violence*. There has been much more of it than can be *justified,* and even more than was *necessary* for the conquest and preservation of a *monopoly* of power.

The following distinction made by Peter Berger is critical:

> In asking about the human costs of revolution, it is also very important to distinguish between those costs resulting from revolutionary warfare and those exacted by a revolutionary regime that has attained power. Both in terms of

practical necessity and of possible moral justification, there is a great difference between acts of terror undertaken against armed (and possibly equally
terroristic) opponents, and terror imposed on opponents who have been dis-
armed and are fully under the control of a revolutionary regime. This distinction is at the basis of whatever progress has been made in recent centuries in
the international law of war. It applies equally, and for exactly the same reasons, to the warfare of revolutionary movements. [12]

Indeed, the *real* opportunities for the humanization of revolution arise only
when the armed struggle with counterrevolution has come to an end. The revolution's relationship toward its vanquished enemy is a realistic test of revolutionary humanism.

Violence is not a neutral instrument. People characterize their goals and
their own nature in the manner in which they apply it. Man is an indivisible
whole. He who acts without any self-imposed limits toward his enemy will easily turn violence against his comrade-in-arms. In the hands of Stalin and his
followers, violence got out of control as early as during the collectivization of
the countryside, and not only when they began to murder their own comrades.
The Stalinists understood class war and "dekulakization" as the physical annihilation of an entire social group.

No Marxist can be permitted to draw the veil over Lenin's decision to permit
the murder of the Tsar's entire family, not even *excluding the children*. [13] To be
sure, this was in the midst of a civil war, when there was a danger that foreign
interventionists would try to free the Tsar. That Lenin and the other leaders
did not have a clear conscience, however, is shown by the fact that they concealed the full truth from the public and that they pushed it into oblivion.

But how could it have been otherwise, when an entire theodicy had failed to
cope with the suffering of the guiltless, especially the young and frail? This
torment haunted Dostoyevsky, whose Ivan Karamazov reasoned thus: "Why,
the whole world of knowledge is not worth that child's prayer to 'dear, king
God'!"; "and if the sufferings of children go to swell the sum of sufferings
which was necessary to pay for truth, then I protest that the truth is not worth
such a price." [14]

Thus the tradition of revolutionary terrorism in Russia boasted of the efforts
of assassins to avoid at all costs the murder of women and children. This
theme is beautifully developed in Camus' drama, *Les justes*.

The Bolsheviks, however, made neglect of this historical tradition into a virtue. Stalinism expanded the notion of *collective responsibility* to the Bolsheviks themselves, and not only were the "culprits" persecuted and murdered,
but also their children, their wives, relatives, friends, acquaintances. . . .

* * *

When ideologized Marxism becomes dominant in communist parties, they are
made incapable of applying to themselves one of the most important elements of

classical Marxism—its teaching concerning ideology. They have thus remained ignorant of the real forces driving many of their own members.

"Distorted" consciousness always perceives noble or at least acceptable motives behind the actions of its own social group while seeking to identify special interests and other selfish motives in the actions of other groups. Instead of trying to delve more deeply into the motives of its own adherents, this type of Marxism crowns itself with the aura of science and simply scorns all other points of view as modes of "distorted" consciousness. This weakness has been noted by many, among them Max Weber: "We shall not be deceived by this verbiage; the materialist conception of history is no cab to be taken at will; it does not stop short of the promoters of revolutions."[15]

Marx's conception of ideology is only sketched out in his works. Anyone wishing to construct a theory on the basis of that sketch must, among other things, rely upon the achievements of modern psychology. He must uncover the specific psychological processes that mediate between group interests and individuals' pictures of the world, enhancing those interests and distorting those pictures. Marxists have lost much ground in this respect because Stalinism made in-depth and social psychology into taboo subjects.

If through its conception of ideology classical Marxism directed the attention of revolutionaries to the deeper dispositional and motivational layers of the personality, it also had the opposite effect by virtue of two weaknesses.

First, Marx's anthropology was excessively optimistic. Marx knew that man is not only a creative, social, and free being, but also a destructive, selfish, and unfree being. Marx's *conceptual* apparatus did not, however, enable him to attribute equal importance to the latter set of human properties as to the former. In Marx the first set falls into the category of human "essence," whereas the second is included merely in human "existence." Historical experience and science show that man, *precisely in his essence,* bears both of these opposite potentials.

Far more can be learned about the inhumane side of human nature from a Schopenhauer, Nietzsche, or Freud than from Marx. From them we know that the higher are values in a hierarchy, the less are they motivational in character and the greater is their rationalizing role. But in communist parties, in contrast, their own benevolence was seen to serve as a guarantee of the success of the revolutionary-humanist program.

Secondly, classical Marxism diminished the role of the leader, although as it turned out leaders were to call the tune within communist parties. In a thematic cycle of revolution as a profession, the first position would belong to those revolutionaries who were subordinated to the machinery of the Third International, particularly once it was Stalinized. In such circumstances, "natural" selection propelled to the top individuals inclined toward authoritarianism and violence.

Quite fortunately, Marx the investigator often broke away from the framework which he defined for himself as a theorist. His critique of primitive communism, for instance, is incomparably more important than his depiction of the generic nature of man in illuminating the dispositions and motivations of human actors, as illustrated by the following passage:

> It may be said that this idea of the *community of women* gives away the *secret* of this as yet completely crude and thoughtless communism. . . . In negating the *personality* of man in every sphere, this type of communism is really nothing but the logical expression of private property, which is this negation. General *envy* constituting itself as a power is the disguise in which *avarice* re-establishes itself, only in *another* way. The thoughts of every piece of private property—inherent in each piece as such—are *at least* turned against all *wealthier* private property in the form of envy and the urge to reduce to a common level, so that this envy and urge even constitute the essence of competition. The crude communist is only the consummation of this envy and of this levelling-down proceeding from the *preconceived* minimum. It has a *definite, limited* standard.[16]

In the depths of this primitive-communist urge for levelling, Marx grasped envy at work. But life has shown that a communism moved by envy produces the opposite effect as well: aping of the wealth, power, and life style of the vanquished ruler and the overthrown ruling classes once communists of this type themselves become the wielders of power. Instead of undertaking exclusively affirmative measures for improving the social composition of the intelligentsia, this kind of regime imposes restrictions motivated by vengeance, for example barring young people of the former exploiting classes from entering higher education.

Since they perceive themselves as the vanguard, communist parties have always displayed deep concern regarding the social origins of their members. Those members who come from the possessing and power-holding classes are submitted to particular scrutiny. But the problem is that there is a psychological complex not only of wealth and power, but also of poverty and powerlessness. The former usually gives rise to feelings of guilt and self-punishment through asceticism and egalitarianism, while the latter generates envy and the urge to put oneself in the position of the wealthy and powerful.

In such parties it is unheard of to make distinctions between actual and latent inclinations, as well as among conscious, semiconscious, and unconscious motivations. It has been the rare individual who has had the will, the opportunity, and the power to take the precaution of worrying about envy, personal ambition, the will to power, self-love, and the like even during the revolutionary phase. The most fatal omission in this regard was committed by Lenin in choosing Stalin as his closest collaborator. Everyone emphasizes Lenin's far-sightedness when, shortly before his death, he demanded that Stalin be replaced. But what of Lenin's short-sightedness—before?

3. Communist Charisma/rch/y

How is it that communism, as a movement which seeks to abolish the division of society into classes, into state and subjects, leaders and masses, itself becomes distinctly charismatic? This is one of the questions to which this entire book is addressed.

What conception of history and of their own mission is held by *authoritarian* communist parties? The party is seen as the irreplaceable agent of historical progress toward communist society, which is itself conceptualized in an eschatological manner. This exclusive historical mandate is epistemological and axiological, as well as practical-political, in nature. These parties' monopoly on the vanguard role is seen as flowing from their cumulative historical experience and sense of mission. For this reason they are neither willing nor able to function in equal coalitions with other parties and groups.

Such communist parties enjoy the greatest success in environments with strong authoritarian traditions and authoritarian political cultures. After so many centuries of charismatic rulers, it is only natural in such settings that revolutions have brought to power charismatic parties and leaders. These countries have also been known for the markedly patriarchal and religious manner in which the masses are reared. Nor is the low cultural level of the population a negligible factor.

Anyone wishing to investigate communist charisma must proceed from the results of the well-known psychological and socio-psychological studies of the authoritarian personality. Identification with a charismatic collective dominated by a leader who is portrayed as the gift of history provides substantial compensation for individual powerlessness: "He is strengthened: he sees himself as part of something vast, powerful, unified."[17] The sensation of superiority over those who do not enjoy the privilege of belonging to the Party is more than adequate compensation for one's own subordination to the Party. The aura of charisma falls upon each adherent, even the most ordinary: ". . . his consciousness of his very self was abruptly erased and then he began to be painfully aware of the piercing sensation that he was storing up in his heart the reflections of a force that was truly overwhelming him but which was worthy of boundless love and respect."[18] Love of leaders is manifested as veneration, fervor, adoration, zeal, devotion. . . .

The leader of the charismatic party, just like the ordinary member, has the feeling of being in the service of history, but he also feels that he is in *personal* collaboration with history. The charismarch[19] is above the party. Therefore he does not hesitate to impose his will by force when he is in the minority, for, according to him, the number of votes is less important than the interests of the working class.[20] He also permits himself to neglect convening party congresses or arbitrarily to alter the policies affirmed under his leadership at previous ones, openly declaring that the congresses were wrong.

As forcefully as they have tried to accelerate the course of history in their realms, communist parties and leaders have just as rapidly and *spontaneously* become charismatic in the eyes of the people. In a short period of time some of these parties, from small revolutionary groups, become numerous and strong revolutionary organizations which proceed to liberate their country from foreigners, seize power, and carry out radical social changes.

Thus did the Bolshevik Party, in a mere twenty years, traverse the path from a revolutionary sect to the ruler of one-sixth of the globe. The Chinese Communist Party, which was founded by twelve individuals in 1921, was victorious in a civil war just twenty-eight years later. And in Fidel Castro we have an example of a revolutionary who achieved charismatic authority before he became a communist. In the summer of 1953 Castro and 126 followers rushed the Moncada barracks. Seventy of them perished and the rest were seized. After he was later amnestied, Castro went into foreign exile and then with 82 comrades carried out an "invasion" of Cuba. Apart from twelve who succeeded in escaping into the mountains, all the rest were killed. On the first of January 1959, only six years after the adventure at the Moncada, Castro entered Havana at the head of a revolutionary army.

The cumulative social balance of a particular instance of charisma can be neither positive or negative; this is a matter for concrete study in each individual case. The only general conclusion that is warranted is that the strength of a particular charisma is always in direct relation to the magnitude of political poverty. The root of charisma must be sought in the existence of a mass that is inclined to be shaped and led. In Marxist terms, charisma is a typically "prehistorical" phenomenon. Societies with communist charisma merely represent a difficult transition to the post-charismatic age, but in no sense a transition from "prehistory" to "history" as the ruling ideology claims.

One of the most interesting aspects of the creation of a leader cult is the relationship between spontaneity and premeditation. It is a commonplace of social science that great leaders spontaneously acquire charismatic traits in times of social crisis and revolution. There is no better example of this than Lenin's cult. Almost all of Lenin's acquaintances noted his lack of vanity and his numerous sincere and resolute protests against the exaltation of his personal merits. The communist party leaders who followed him, however, gladly relied on the propagation of their cults by the party or the party-state apparatus.

The fabrication of Stalin's cult is of interest to the investigator for a number of reasons. Here we come across the rare phenomenon of one great cult immediately following upon another. Stalin elevated himself under the wing of Lenin's cult, transforming Lenin's grave into a sanctuary and his statements (as interpreted by Stalin) into verdicts on all questions. Thus in the cultivation of the cults of both Lenin and Stalin, planned actions increasingly pushed the spontaneous needs and experience of the masses into the background. In Stalin's case it was also demonstrated that autocrats with great theoretical ambitions but little talent for theoretical creativity are fatal to intellectual life.

It is not one of the lesser ironies of history that the Bolshevik Party concentrated on the "danger" of Trotsky instead of defending itself against Stalin's ambitions. To be sure, Trotsky's charisma had long been in operation, while Stalin's was just being born. In undertaking to curb Trotsky's allegedly Bonapartist intentions, many failed to recognize Stalin's craving for power. And Trotsky acted like an arrogant intellectual full of illusions about the strength of reason in the clash with the will of steel and with the power apparatus at its disposition. Stalin's genius for manipulation and organization made his victory all the easier. And that Trotsky underestimated Stalin should be no surprise, insofar as his assessment of Lenin was condescending up to 1917 itself.

The outcome of the struggle between Stalin and Trotsky, as well as of the struggle between the corresponding Party currents and social forces, offers an appropriate opportunity for posing the question of the *relationship between collective and individual charisma*. In Trotsky's fall from power he was the victim of, among other things, the illusion that his charisma had a prospect of winning ascendancy over the collective charisma of the Party to which Stalin "humbly" appealed and with the help of which he sought to prop himself up. To this point no one had exploited the Party's charisma in the establishment of personal charisma so successfully as Stalin. In the end, nearly the entire charisma of the Party was transferred, incarnated, and concentrated in Stalin's person.

Lenin was not disturbed by Trotsky's charisma. At that time the cumulative amount of charisma was not very great and there were still other Bolsheviks who were leaders in their own right. While the Party did not really share power with anyone else, internally its charismatic authority was divided among several personalities.

Stalin eliminated all competition for charismatic power. Close consideration of the manner in which he eliminated Trotsky's influence reveals one point of general significance. In clashes with charismatic rivals, the most effective are usually those who do not attempt to deny their rivals' charismatic qualities directly, but who instead "merely" transform these rivals in the eyes of the masses into *bearers of negative charisma*. The "Stalin generations" were reared to see in Trotsky the incarnation of counterrevolution. Both positive and negative charisma equally enter into the Stalinist mythology of the October Revolution.

Under Khrushchev, the vengeance of history began to catch up with Stalin posthumously. In the name of Lenin's charisma, Stalin's acquired in large part a negative quality. The ejection of Stalin's corpse from Lenin's mausoleum graphically symbolized that process.

For the investigator it is not of great intellectual interest to follow the fabrication of the cults of the East European leaders, on whom Stalin conferred a portion of his power and the right to create their own cults, albeit in the shadow of his supreme cult. While Stalin's charisma spontaneously relied, to a certain extent, on his participation in the leadership of the October Revolution, the cults of the East European party chieftans were totally fabricated. This is why they were so short-lived.

The connections between the birth of charisma and the masses' craving for release from social crisis have been rather thoroughly researched. But investigation of the reverse phenomenon has been virtually ignored: the role of the charismatic leader in the provocation—both spontaneously and premeditatedly—of crisis.

A leader may gain charismatic power by dispelling a social crisis, but later, as an *autocrat,* he can erect formidable impediments to social development. At this point he begins to add one palliative measure after another to his political rosary. The boundary condition obtains when his positive charisma is transformed into negative charisma within his lifetime. Charisma, too, has inertia: the leader's position is such that he must rule even after his abilities to solve social problems have eroded or disappeared, for the cult itself is a first-order material force in his hands.[21]

Still, the autocrat must reinvigorate and prove his charisma from time to time. "Hence a wise prince must adopt a policy which will insure that his citizens always and in all circumstances will have need of his government; then they will always be faithful to him."[22] In order to preserve his role as society's savior, the autocrat can resort to stimulating tensions, disagreements, and conflicts within the party-state hierarchy. When this leads to political crisis he will, as it were, use "Caesarean" section to remove the culprits, real or imaginary. The hand weaving the intrigues becomes visible only when they become unwoven. This political game is shrouded from the ordinary citizen.

The autocrat will be careful not to overdo his attacks on one side of the hierarchy lest he become dependent on the other. An excessively radical prophylaxis might smother the conception of future tensions and disagreements. The study of conflict in such societies is not very promising unless one takes the role of the charismatic autocrat as one's point of departure.

In order to preserve his supremacy until the end of his life, the autocrat must be a very skilled ruler, but not so skilled as is ordinarily assumed. It is not at all difficult when he maintains his grasp on *all* the levers of power and influence from earlier days—the party, the state administration, the army, police, and propaganda machinery. . . . If necessary he can turn directly to the masses. So long as all the reins are divided and they all rest ultimately in his hands alone, the autocrat's exceptional position is in no danger.

No social order is well served if it lacks the strength to treat its leader as a human, limited being and allows him to become independent and arrogant. In such societies monuments are erected to living leaders, they are vowed "unreserved loyalty," and "definitive" assessments are promulgated concerning their historical role. But *"our roles are always future.* They appear to each one as tasks to be performed, ambushes to be avoided, powers to be exercised, etc."[23] Like all other human beings, the leader represents a potential source of evil as well as good as long as he lives. Therefore, "not one human creature merits the belief that he rules until death! Regardless of the ideas he advocates, regardless of the nature of the movement he represents or the qualities he possesses. . . ."[24]

But it is worth little to have a heightened sensitivity to all this if, apart from the charismatic autocrat himself, no strong institutions are allowed to take root. In this case the general feeling of anxiety about the future without the charismatic helmsman is only magnified. It is most humiliating for a society to believe that its fate depends upon a biological contingency.

These are the kinds of situations in which the party-state hierarchy struggles to survive the whims of its charismatic leader, fearing for his death while at the same time secretly wishing it. Even that very political summit which had so loyally and diligently exalted its leader becomes the prisoner of his cult. Apart from the irony of the situation, however, there is a certain justice in it as well! All that remains for this summit is merely to outdo itself in the leader's glorification. Anyone who falters in this effort will fall under the blows of the leader's mistrust and vanity. If anyone displays impatience in maneuvering for the charismarch's inheritance or attempts to position himself so as to be named the successor by the charismarch himself, he will most likely be removed from the political stage. But when the charismarch dies, the former stage set is destroyed and the new one is indicative of quite different relationships, coalitions, and powers.

Very little has been done toward the study of the true role of the leader in societies which call themselves socialist. In so far as the need for such research is obvious, the real reason for its paucity is to be found not in the intellectual powerlessness of scholars residing in these societies, but rather in the power of their leaders.

4. The Statist Revolution in the USSR

The enormous renunciations imposed by War Communism were bound to lead, sooner or later, to an impasse. Camus would have put it this way: "The day comes when ideology clashes with psychology."[25] Here is what Zinoviev had to say in this regard at the height of War Communism: "It is useless to deny that many militants are mortally weary . . . excessive mental strain is demanded; they are sent here to-day and there to-morrow by the Party or by chance; the result is inevitably psychological exhaustion."[26]

In these circumstances Lenin sought salvation in the New Economic Policy (NEP). The NEP was much less a relaxation in politics than it was in economics. The Tenth Congress of the Bolshevik Party in 1921 adopted NEP at the same time as it promulgated the ban on factions. The Kronstadt uprising also certainly contributed to the anxiety within the Bolsheviks' ranks. Radek described the dilemma confronting the Party in the following way:

> We are now at the point where the workers, at the end of their endurance, refuse any longer to follow a vanguard which leads them to battle and sacrifice. . . . Ought we to yield to the clamors of the workingmen who have reached the limit of their patience but who do not understand their true interests as we do? Their state of mind is at present frankly reactionary. But the Party has decided that we must *not* yield, that we must impose our will to victory on our exhausted and dispirited followers.[27]

In the period immediately following the October Revolution, several parties were permitted to exist and the Left Social Revolutionaries participated in the government. All this, to be sure, came to an early end, although at least in the Bolshevik Party a considerable amount of freedom existed. In its long-term consequences, the Tenth Congress proved to be fatal for intra-party democracy.

Even before the Tenth Congress, workers' self-management had been replaced by individual management. Just as Lenin had previously so naively considered in *State and Revolution* that laymen could resolve all the important questions of management, so, shortly after the October Revolution, did he facilely conclude that these questions ought to be left to managers.[28]

One solution, at the same time democratic and realistic, was possible providing that a distinction were made between two domains.[29] The first consists of the selection of adequate resources, the day-to-day guidance of economic affairs, and other professional questions. But the second is comprised of the establishment of goals and of general directions, and other social questions. A modern economy can function only if the first domain is entrusted to qualified managers. But if a society is to be fit for living, self-management should be situated in the second domain. In their primitive insistence that self-management must be unlimited, some of the adherents of the Workers' Opposition merely played into the hands of the advocates of unlimited managerial control. It is worth noting, in passing, that individual management in the economy and individual leadership in politics are mutually reinforcing and strengthening factors.

Of what consequence was it that Lenin, toward the end of his life, warned with alarm of political and economic centralization and bureaucratization, once he had become increasingly entangled in all sorts of superficial countermeasures? The usurpation of the party-state apparatus could have been halted at that point only by radical moves, and in the long term only through democratic institutional reforms.

Nor did Bolshevik ideology exactly provide grounds for encouragement in the search for such solutions. Its two underlying principles were *proletarian dictatorship* and *democratic centralism*. In the case of these principles we can observe how ideological "distortion" occurs even during the phase of assigning names to concepts. This power is based on a prior assumption of naive linguistic realism on the part of the broad masses, who are deemed unable to draw sufficiently clear distinctions between a word and that which it denominates.

In a language undeformed by ideology, the "dictatorship" and "centralism" referred to above would simply be described as "revolutionary." Then the question of their proletarian and democratic content would remain empirical and open. Bolshevik ideologists, however, established an *a priori and analytical* connection between "dictatorship" and "proletariat," and between "centralism" and "democracy." In this manner, the ideology suppressed the reality of party dictatorship and the undemocratic aspects of party centralism. Even more disturbing, Bolshevik ideology was potentially *conservative* from the very beginning: if the dictatorship was *by definition* proletarian and the centralism *by definition* democratic, it followed that it was senseless to make any demands for the proletarianization of the dictatorship or for the democratization of centralism.

In squaring accounts with Trotsky and the entire Left Opposition, Stalin skillfully exploited the need of the masses for a long breathing spell after the War Communism period. The prospect of returning to a time of extreme renunciation under a policy of "primitive socialist accumulation" was truly attractive only to a very few. It is often claimed that Stalin basically appropriated the Left Opposition's platform once he had eliminated it from the political arena. Yet the Left Opposition was opposed, for instance, to renewed introduction of terror and to privileges for the party-state apparatus—and were these really trivial differences?

Instead of primitive socialist accumulation, there was created *primitive statist accumulation*. These events are commonly referred to as "the new revolution," "the revolution from above," or "the revolution within a revolution." But what was the social content of the Stalinist Revolution?

This was a *statist revolution*. The entirety of social life—from agriculture and industry, through politics, and as far as culture—was brought under the control of the state. There remained not a single social institution which the supercentralized party-state apparatus did not transform into its "transmission belt." The Workers' Opposition supported the revolution of the proletariat against "its own" bureaucracy. The Third Revolution, in contrast, abolished the last remaining rights of the working class. It was one of the bloodiest revolutions in history. A new class society—statism, with its own ruling class—a statist class which collectively owned the means of production, was created. In my previous book I have elaborated this position in considerable detail.

The new ruling class rapidly abandoned the pauperistic strain of communism and began to live in a particularistic, hedonistic, and privileged manner. At the same time the bulk of the working class, the peasantry, and the intelligentsia were made to live collectivistically, ascetically, and in an egalitarian manner.[30] Statist ideologists attempted to justify these differences by citing Marx's critique of primitive communism. As early as 1931 Stalin, in the name of the principle of distribution according to work, openly abandoned *uravni-lovka*. But while levelling egalitarianism and levelling asceticism were disavowed early on, the principle of collectivism has remained one of the *ideological* pillars of statism to this day. I say "ideological" because the ideologists of statism preach collectivism as the regulative principle of society as a whole while the statist class acts and rules in conformity with its own interests.

It has long been noted that the capitalist class does not wish to be called a "class." So, too, with the statist class, except that it actually wishes to represent itself as a component part of the subjugated class, the working class.

The Bolsheviks maintained that in Russia the bourgeoisie was too weak to consummate the bourgeois-democratic revolution and that it had to be replaced in this capacity by the working class, which would then try forthwith to deepen the revolution and to transform it into a socialist revolution. Among Marxists the most popular explanation for the triumph of Stalinism is that the working class, as a consequence of its small size and its exhaustion, was incapable of consummating and preserving the socialist revolution. In fact, however, the working class lacked the strength even to consolidate the legacy of the bourgeois-democratic revolution. Thus there was established a statist order in which it did not enjoy even those rights for which it had struggled under capitalism—wage negotiation, changing of one's workplace, the freedom to strike and of association. . . .

There are serious Marxists who, while denying that the USSR can be at all characterized as a socialist society, nevertheless define it as a society "of the transitional period to socialism." I would immediately make the following two observations. First, the idea of the "transitional period" has hitherto more often been abused to justify the weaknesses of ruling communist parties than utilized as a stimulus to critical analysis of their rule. Secondly, the above formula in and of itself is meaningless, for every period is a transition between two other periods; the question is "merely" one of what is really in transition.

A half century has passed since the onset of the Stalinist Revolution and the contours of the system that issued from that revolution have long since become clear. How long will Marxists continue to treat it as an entirely temporary phenomenon that is the namesake of a desired future? How much longer must we wait for that system to merit its own name? Such treatment belongs to the realm of ideology sooner than to that of science.

If we call a system statist, this naturally need not imply the absence of any socialist elements in it. Contemporary capitalism also has such elements, yet no Marxist would characterize it as the "transitional period to socialism." The Marxists whom I criticize here believe that the existence of state ownership of the means of production demonstrates the socialist character of the USSR's "economic base," in contrast to the "political superstructure" which is said to be "bureaucratic." But it is insupportable to identify state ownership with social ownership and to proceed further in taking this to constitute the basis of socialism. If the entire society (with the exception of the state apparatus) is excluded from the control and disposition of property, then the true character of that property and ownership is concealed and mystified by calling them "social."

* * *

The statists of today live and act in a kind of middle world. They incessantly insinuate themselves into the life of society, but between their true effectiveness and their self-image there gapes an enormous chasm. In mass sociopolitical organizations, the professional apparatus is preoccupied with itself. The illusion of close ties with society is created for it by workers, collective farmers, intellectuals, women, and youth whom it itself has selected to represent society. In this markedly political society, political poverty is the overwhelming rule for the masses.

Despite its isolation, the political apparatus is extraordinarily vain and nearly all of its measures and meetings are proclaimed to be of historical importance. Naturally, the greater the real historical accomplishments, the lesser is the need for an escalation of historical pretenses and for ideological-political static in general.

The statists remain rather boastful in times of crisis as well. In such circumstances they criticize the existing state of things from a pseudo-objective distance, as if what is at issue is some sort of spontaneous development in which they had no part or responsibility. Instead of lowering their voices they become more vocal than ever with their fatalistic optimism, which is so perfectly registered in the satirical aphorism, "The past constantly changes, but that is why the future is completely certain."

Their "newspeak" is a story unto itself. No one more than they and the propagandists in their service has so corrupted the language of the region they inhabit. At times language gives us the power "that through magical lyrics and incantations we can cast even the moon from the heavens."[31] The statists do not get so carried away. Their speech is primarily of an anesthetic character. A second basic function of that speech is political and ritualistic. It is a language of password and countersign. Unless certain designated words are utilized, the statist remains naked to the attacks of his rivals.

Anyone determined to compile their political syntagm would have a small job before him, but for the same reason a compilation of their antisyntagm would be very rich indeed. Koestler once wrote about a young man whose enemy was able to recognize him as a communist after he had made repeated use of the word "concretely." There is a whole range of stereotypical expressions which exposes the majority of statists. Their political practice is also "enriched" by new names for old phenomena. Through neologisms there is created the appearance of dynamic movement, masking the failure of previous policies.

The statists have pronounced need of a moralistic ideology.[32] This moralism was given official status with the adoption of "The Moral Code of the Builder of Communism" at the Twenty-Second Congress of the Communist Party of the Soviet Union in 1961. To this day, this morality has remained totally subordinate to politics. A glance at the aforementioned Moral Code suffices to confirm the general impression of heteronomy and conformism. The individual must subordinate himself in all things to society, which is identified with the state, and the state in turn with the Party. "Injustice," "dishonesty," "parasitism," etc., are discussed only as individual defects unrelated to the social system, social relations, and social institutions. This moral digest enumerates the *obligations* of the individual toward the community, but not those of the community toward the individual. There is not a single mention of any *rights* of man. The society of "developed socialism" has gone so far as to rehearse the old Christian principle, "He who does not work, need not eat."

Stalin considered that the class struggle intensifies during the development of socialism. This assessment is now officially rejected, but it keeps coming back to life in modified forms. There is not a single known form of social or political conflict of any consequence that would be acknowledged in statism as *"socialist by nature."* Feelings of fear bordering on panic are evident whenever serious disagreements and conflicts come to the surface. Judging by the frequency of attacks on the "enemies of socialism," these phenomena are becoming increasingly common, even though it is officially asserted that there are only a "handful" of such individuals and that they are "being held in check and are harmless." And when persecution of these "enemies" creates a picture of a markedly repressive situation, that situation is proclaimed to be the concoction of those enemies themselves. We know that the struggle against the "enemies of socialism" is most often inversely proportional to the true struggle for socialism. Not a single step forward is feasible until the slogan, "He who is not with us is against us," is replaced at least with the invitation, "He who is not against us is with us."

Statism has long been a fetter on economic development, both industrial and agricultural. Technologically, not only has it failed to "catch up with and overtake" the most developed capitalist countries; it has fallen farther behind them. While excessive centralization is favorable to the domination of the ethnic Russian element, it exacerbates the national question. For science, philosophy, art, and creativity in general, statism is a most unfavorable environment.

Its dynamic elements have yet to be made sufficiently apparent. One thing is for certain: urgent reforms are essential. Judging from all we know, the most that can be expected in the near future is a certain amount of decentralization in economic decision-making and greater utilization of market mechanisms. The possibility should also not be excluded of elementary forms of worker and peasant participation in the management of industrial enterprises and of state and collective farms.

For the time being, the prospects for more serious political liberalization, not to speak of political democratization, are slight. In this respect we ought to figure on decades of difficult struggle in the coming years. After all, the democratization of capitalism, too, required a drawn-out period of effort and for this reason claimed many victims. So long as statism was able to legitimize itself to some extent by invoking the October Revolution and socialism, it was on the ideological offense against capitalism. Recently, however, the countries of democratic capitalism, upholding the cause of civil and human rights, have thrown it completely on an ideological defensive from which there appears to be no relief.

5. Maoism Against Revolutionary Entropy

Once its leaders come to power, every revolution begins to be seized by entropy. "The law of revolution—it is purple, burning, death-giving; but this death is for the sake of the beginning of a new life, for the sake of a star. But the law of entropy is cold, blue as ice, as the icy interplanetary infinity. The flame turns from purple to pink, stabilized, warm, not death-giving but comforting; the sun ages into a planet benign to roads, salesgirls, beds, prostitutes, prisons: this is the law. And for the planet to be rekindled with youth, it has to be rekindled with fire, it has to be forced off the harmonious path of evolution: this is the law."[33]

The revolution aroused the masses from their lethargy: how to prevent them from becoming passive once again? Everyday life threatens to transform the revolution into a short-lived occurrence: what can be done to prevent the political revolution from swallowing up the social revolution? Exhausted on the long journey to the end of the revolutionary rainbow, confronted with the chasm between will and energy, there are many who lament, "Why is it that the bourgeois revolution was such a rapid success while the socialist revolution has resulted in a series of crises?"[34] It is small comfort that the socialist revolution was conceived as the product of hope in the end of class "prehistory" and the beginning of humanity's real history.

All these problems simply obsessed Mao Tse-tung, particularly during the last fifteen years or so of his life. Late Maoism found a counterweight to revolutionary entropy in the *restoration of pauperistic communism*. This kernel of the revolutionary tradition, which emerged in its purest form during the Hunan-Kiangsi and Yenan period, is a *qualitative* absolute for Maoist ideology. And when the profile of the Maoist revolutionary would come to permeate Chinese society as a whole, that kernel would become a *quantitative absolute* as well, and thus would the communist future be achieved.

Maoists, in a peculiar sense, seek utopia in the revolutionary past rather than in the future.[35] Socialism, in their view, is a "transitional period" to the communist past. Seen from the perspective of the Cultural Revolution, the "lower phase of communism" is fulfilled in the long march in which one must overcome suffering in order to abandon oneself to an ascetic and egalitarian collectivism.

In an earlier time, the Maoists were in the habit of justifying the renunciations demanded of the Chinese on the basis of the happiness of future generations. Although such sacrifice was not lacking in *meaning,* it was in conflict with the principle of *justice.* This was not a matter of the inevitable historical injustice inherent in the fact that the new generations always enjoy the privilege of reaping the fruits of the efforts of the previous generations; rather, the question was merely one of whether the terrible burden of exertion might not be more even if it were distributed among several generations of Chinese. Nor was an asceticism of purely *instrumental* value particularly suitable in terms of disputing the policies of the Soviet Communist Party, which recognized the rights of its citizens to the higher standard of living made possible through the sacrifices of earlier generations. The USSR could not plausibly be reproached merely on the grounds that it was not prepared to forego a higher standard of living for the sake of lessening the onus borne by the Chinese people.

In the course of the Cultural Revolution there emerged a tendency toward the ideological absolutization of asceticism. It was as if there was something *intrinsically* bad about pleasure and *intrinsically* good about self-denial and as if pleasure inevitably led back to capitalism. While this eliminated the aforementioned difficulties about justice, there was created in return a crisis of meaning with regard to the concept of self-denial. Since self-denial was expected of all generations, past and future, it was obliged to spin circles around itself in search of meaning in and of itself.

The Maoists have indicted the USSR for imposing material incentives for work and abandoning moral incentives. Moralism or economism—this is the ostensible difference between the lands of pauperistic communism and those of consumer communism. This classification is, of course, only relative in so far as the "consumer" brand of communism in many respects resembles pauperistic communism when compared with the standard of living in the West.

But again we are witness to an ideological struggle rather than to a true conflict of ideas. Both sides possess severely distorted views of reality. In none of these countries—apart from Yugoslavia, which cares nothing for "moral" incentives—is the question *really* posed in disjunctive form. In so far as both forms of incentive are practiced, that is to say, the difference is more one of degree than of principle.

Not even at the height of the Cultural Revolution in China was the system abandoned whereby blue-collar workers are divided into eight pay categories and white-collar workers into fourteen, while functionaries and officers, particularly the highest, as well as the most essential scientists, are given far greater rewards than the rest of the population.

As for the USSR, although it is known for its greater social stratification, its distributive system tends to suppress incentive to a considerable degree. Its shortcomings are supposed to be compensated through moral recognition for those who contribute more than their share, but this is generally ineffective. Such is the case when, for instance, in developing criteria for distribution according to work it often happens that everything but output enters into the equation. While there are plenty of wage gradations, wages themselves are more or less fixed. When output is measured, it is done adequately enough with respect to individuals, but not with respect to enterprises. Poor work collectives find the shelter of the centralistic-distributive economy benign to them as well. It is no wonder that productivity in the USSR lags so far behind that of the West, that operations are irrational, and that the squandering of resources and absenteeism are so widespread. And once one earns a decent wage it often turns out that there is nothing to spend it on, since large-scale consumer-oriented production has been neglected. And China finds itself confronted with these torments with a vengeance.

Since the action of material interests — both personal and group interests — is unavoidable, it would be best for socialism to take greater account of them. Otherwise these interests will be cruelly avenged by the communist moralizers, who would goad people to labor without introducing the principle of distribution according to work under the illusion that by means of this shortcut they can create the New Man.

Yet from Marx they might learn that whenever ideas have been compromised in the course of history it is because they were not reinforced by interest, and that morality becomes powerless in action unless it proceeds from people as they are. For these reasons Marx counted on the interests of the proletariat instead of its altruism. He did, to be sure, criticize capitalism for being based on heedless private interest. This did not, however, prevent him from proclaiming capitalism to be a more progressive form of social organization than any other that had been based on extra-economic dependence and compulsion.

To what degree is the type of incentive which figures as "moral" incentive in the dispute between the Chinese and Soviet communist parties truly moral? Were it the case that the Chinese work not for gain but exclusively out of enthusiasm and the desire to contribute to social progress, we would indeed be concerned here with a selfless morality of work. But it is difficult for even the Maoists themselves to believe that they are surrounded by such "heroes of labor." It is rather more likely that the attitude of the Chinese toward work is governed more by the desire to avoid the condemnation of their milieu or to earn its favor.

But if the main components of that milieu which one *must* take into account are the party, the state, and repressive institutions and situations, then are we speaking of morality at all? The Maoists went so far as to make the size of one's wage dependent upon one's political activity as well. Consequently, a substantial portion of one's motivation to work was at best *political*, not moral. Why should work under duress (of whatever form) be more morally acceptable than work for monetary gain? A society which educates its members to work solely for gain cultivates selfishness. But Maoist "moral" stimulation encourages conformism. Just about all that the Maoists achieved by imposing morality at the expense of the economy is that they made politics dominant. Were the economy truly based on morality, the Maoists would have had no need for so many political campaigns[36] to ensure its functioning.

In spite of all this, a communism with an explicitly consumerist orientation would in no sense represent a real solution for contemporary China. Such a materially backward society would have no real hope were it not prepared to set today's bread aside for tomorrow. But neither does China's solution lie in the absolutization of ascetic communism. Yet it was precisely in this direction that the needle of the ideological compass was pointing during the Cultural Revolution. It is bad enough when a virtue is made of necessity, but it is even worse when it is proclaimed an absolute virtue. Paraphrasing Marx, we might say that social revolution cannot draw its poetry from past, not even—we might add—from its own past, but rather from the future.

In any event, China now faces the task of modernization. In no way would it be constructive, however, for the gradual improvement of the standard of living of each individual regardless of his or her labor contribution, or for the principle of equalization of opportunities for education, medical care, etc. to fall under the blows of modernization. But at the same time it would be constructive if, along with this basic equality, there were developed adequate material incentives for productivity and creativity, and if on that basis the enjoyment of a more comfortable life were encouraged.

The Cultural Revolution was not the Maoists' first attempt to absolutize pauperistic communism. The same was intended, although less explicitly, in the unsuccessful "Great Leap Forward." Marx better than anyone else understood how indispensable are the economic preconditions of socialism. Leninism turned to the political organization of revolutionaries as the decisive factor. But Maoism even further distanced itself from the "economic base" in seeking the lever in the spiritual sphere—conscience and will. It is an elementary tenet of Maoism that even "social class" is more an ideological than an economic category. It is from here that such great emphasis in Maoism is placed upon re-education, criticism and self-criticism, and propaganda.

Sensing that opportunities for class stratification would be generated spontaneously, Mao warned that China needed countermeasures on the order of the Cultural Revolution every twenty years. But he was thoroughly mistaken in thinking that just this insistence on the pauperistic side of communism could create a lasting immunity against class differentiation.

Periodic revolutionary campaigns would not have sufficed to sustain continued collectivistic and ascetic egalitarianism. These measures would have had to become increasingly more severe. But in this way the pretorians of pauperistic communism would only have turned into its gravediggers.

Oscar Wilde once remarked, "There is only one class in the community that thinks more about money than the rich, and that is the poor. They can think of nothing else."[37] And George Orwell said that the poor seldom praise poverty. In order to stamp out their desire for comfort it would have been necessary to apply ever more reckless amounts of coercion. It would not have been the first time that increasingly large gaps in society were opened up under the pretext of preserving the revolution: a repressive apparatus would have hounded the masses to live ascetically while it itself enjoyed privileges of all sorts. Thus would the very frenzy of pauperistic communism have led to its opposite — a new class society.

Mao seems to have had presentiments that his line in the Chinese Communist Party would not long survive: "As he courteously escorted me to the door, he said he was not a complicated man, but really very simple. He was, he said, only a *lone monk* walking the world *with a leaky umbrella*."[38] The farsightedness of this comment was demonstrated by the arrest of his wife and other top Maoists on the day, so to speak, after his death.

It is of course not the purpose of this book to attempt a comprehensive evaluation of Maoism, not even of late Maoism. Yet I should like to address only a few comments to the positions of the Maoist and pro-Maoist faction of the Western Left — of that faction which has glorified the Maoism of the Cultural Revolution.

Chinese collectivism appears very attactive to those leftists who declare their opposition to the egoism of capitalist society. The trouble is, however, that this collectivism has no place for the individual if he deviates even the slightest bit from the collective. "Struggle-criticism-transformation" — all this looks like life in a true community, but only so long as we are unconcerned about whether people become disgraced and degraded.

A great number of people have been very impressed by the participation of the people, especially the youth, in political actions, campaigns, and clashes in China. But the critical mind can distinguish political participation from political freedom. The manipulation of mass dissatisfaction on the part of an untouchable charismarch has nothing in common with democracy.

It is accurate to say that the Cultural Revolution was unprecedented in the entire history of communism. A divinely inspired leader relied on the country's youth and laid seige to his previous source of support — the party-state apparatus — in order, as he explained, to prevent it from becoming a ruling class. Mao took this risk, to be sure, only after he had assured himself of the Army's support. In all these events the toll of human sacrifice was incomparably higher than it appeared from the outside. No one has the right to pass this over with indifference.

Thus Maoism, too, is an authoritarian variety of communism. The fact that the charismarch was so powerful as to dare to strike out at the charisma of the party-state apparatus is of little real consequence.

Mao's position toward the peasantry differed from the customary approach found in Marxism and Leninism. Marx had no sympathy for the peasantry and despised the "idiocy" of its lifestyle. Lenin discovered in the peasantry a great revolutionary potential that could be exploited if it was guided by the industrial proletariat, and the latter by the Party. Borrowing from Kautsky, he considered that class consciousness among the workers must be brought in by intellectuals who have deserted the ruling classes. Mao turned all this around: the workers, and in a sense the peasants to an even greater extent, represent the source not only of inspiration but also of consciousness for the intellectuals and for the Party.

It is well known that the Chinese Communist Party at first imitated to a certain extent the Stalinist model of primitive accumulation based on the exploitation of the countryside and that it adopted the dogma of the absolute priority of industry over agriculture and of heavy industry over all else. The position on the peasantry which he had developed earlier helped Mao to revise this orientation and to decide on a course of more balanced development. Of course the partial economic autonomy of the commune should also be counted to Mao's credit.

Some Western leftists find in the obligatory physical labor of intellectuals and functionaries the beginnings of the elimination of the contradiction between mental and physical labor and between the city and the countryside. Physical labor can be useful in the clash of intellectual and bureaucratic vanities. But to "lower" the intellectual and the functionary to the level of the manual worker does not mean to "raise" the latter to the level of the former. This can be accomplished only through the mechanization and automation of labor, the development of mass education, the participation of the masses in the management of society, and a host of similar measures.

The Maoist slogan of precedence for the "reds" over the "professionals" has an anti-technocratic ring, but it is no less primitive for all that. The replacement of experts by laymen ("reds") must in no way be confused with mass worker and peasant participation in decision-making. As a consequence of declining productivity, irrational organization, lack of work discipline, and so forth the most likely outcome is that the professionals (subordinated, of course, to the politicians) will also appropriate those decisions which in a socialist society ought to be in the competence of workers' and peasants' self-management.

Nor should our eyes be closed to an explicit strain of anti-intellectualism as well. In high culture, art, and social science, Maoism had disastrous results. The upper hand was gained by an intellectual pauperism and nihilism toward world culture and the Chinese cultural edifice, as symbolized by the spectacle of obeisance toward the little red book of the leader's quotations.

As a consequence of their protest against the enslavement to things in the West, some leftists have forgotten that the enslavement to poverty in China is far more onerous. By virtue of their distance from the great consumer centers of the West it is very facile to assert that the Chinese do not share the same desires as everyone else. And those who have been so uncritically impressed by Maoist egalitarianism ought to be instructed to examine how much of this has been reality, and how much ideology.

6. Opportunities for Socialist Democratization – in Yugoslavia

The Communist Party of Yugoslavia led an independent War of National Liberation in the years 1941–45 and succeeded in broadening and deepening that war into a revolution. Upon coming to power it proceeded to construct a new socio-economic system on the model of the USSR. So long as the Party's Stalinist dimension is not acknowledged,[39] it is impossible to understand why it carried over this statist paradigm of social organization into the Yugoslav context.

Stalinism had an extraordinarily strong impact on *all* communist parties. The Third International, at the time a Stalinist transmission belt, confirmed or even installed national party leaderships throughout the world, and Yugoslavia was no exception in this regard.

For these reasons it is especially urgent to subject a whole range of issues in the Party's history to systematic, scientific examination. Among these are the "Bolshevization" (the then current expression for Stalinization) of the CPY, sectarianism within the Party, Party attacks on anti-Stalinist left intellectuals before the war,[40] the crushing of resistance to the Stalinization of the Party, the relationships among the CPY's leaders during the purges in the USSR, and revolutionary terror during the wartime and post-war periods.

The CPY's accomplishment of 1948 was all the greater in that its protagonists had to liberate themselves from both external Stalinism and from their own as well. If the existence of the CPY's Stalinist dimension is denied, there is also no way of explaining the difficult struggle that had to be waged against the Cominformists at even the highest levels of the Party, state, and military.

At times the latent contradiction between the independence of the Yugoslav Revolution and Stalinism's influence on it was bound to develop into overt conflict. After all, to this day there has not been a single independent socialist revolution which has not sooner or later offered resistance to the hegemonistic aspirations of the "international revolutionary center." The potential counter-example of Cuba should not confuse the issue, for Cuba's development would probably have been much more independent were it not for the dangers presented by its proximity to the USA.

From the very beginning, Stalin tried to smash the independence of the Yugoslav Revolution in order to subordinate it to the great-power interests of the USSR. During the war he reprimanded the CPY leadership for leftist sectarianism.[41] It is interesting that Moscow perfidiously induced that same leadership to criticize the communist parties of France and Italy at the first meeting of the Cominform in 1947, thus putting the CPY into the position of unwittingly contributing to its own isolation in the years that were to follow. And in 1948 Stalin accused the Yugoslav leadership of deviations in both directions, albeit more of a leftist than of a rightist character.

The Yugoslav leadership reacted ambivalently to Stalin's charges in 1948. And this was understandable in light of the psychological tendency described by William James: people are unable to accept anything new as true so long as they incorporate it into the stock of existing truths with a *minimum of dissonance* and a *maximum of continuity.* And the CPY leadership indignantly rejected all the charges and proclaimed that it would demonstrate through its actions that it had been slandered.

From this there flowed a series of ultraleftist measures that the CPY would later regret—the nationalization of the last remnants of small-scale trade, services, and weekend cottages; the intensification of policies toward the peasantry through increasingly crude forms of forced procurement of agricultural produce and pressure to enter into peasant work communes;[42] the purge of "bourgeois elements" from the Popular Front. Through this self-criticism in practice the CPY's leaders attempted to prove their loyalty to Stalin[43] and simultaneously to deprive Stalin of all his "arguments" in the belief that with time, they would win.

Thus there was a Stalinist quality to the CPY's resistance to Stalin. How else, indeed, to explain the brutality of the conflict with their comrades-in-arms who had come out for Stalin?

How much can truly be understood and justified on the basis of the size of the stakes and the gravity of the situation in 1948? I believe that future generations will also appreciate that the repression and isolation of the Stalinists was unavoidable. For how much terror would there have been had Stalin succeeded in bringing a Quisling clique to Yugoslavia? Thus there can be no question of any rehabilitation of the real Cominformists. Nevertheless there is no defense for the inhuman conditions and torture in the prisons. And what shall we say of repressive measures employed against the families of Cominformists? And finally there were more than a few who were arrested in haste, completely innocent of any wrongdoing.

The CPY's leaders did not know at the outset how far-reaching their decision to resist Stalin would be. They entered the fray in order to protect their independence and dignity, not out of commitment to any conception of an alternative internal socialist order. The real theoretical groundwork and justification were constructed retrospectively and gradually. The workers' councils, as the touchstone and framework of the new socialism, were created only two years later.

Had the Yugoslav Communists capitulated to Stalin like so many others before and after them, the Yugoslav Revolution of 1941–45 would have been recorded in history as an occurrence of more or less local significance. Events having happened as they did, however, it acquired a world-historical dimension as well. This was the first socialist revolution to break out of the "socialist" (statist) encirclement. Within this encirclement all subsequent attempts at radical change in Eastern Europe were destined to collapse. The Yugoslavs' triumph in their clash with Stalin falls among the most important events of international communism from the October Revolution to the present day.

All this remains indisputable even after one has taken into account the fact that the bearers of the 1948 break later abandoned their own commitment to Stalinism. It is of course true that history is shaped by both objective facts as well as human commitments. Yet some of the leaders of the 1948 break have been inconsistent in retrospect, explaining the conflict with Stalin as the result of their *commitment*, while rationalizing the Stalinist features of their previous policies as deriving from the action of *objective* circumstances.

But in what sense was the period of the terrible political, economic, and military blockade of Yugoslavia on the part of the Eastern bloc more favorable for, say, the creation of workers' councils than the period immediately after the war? It is quite clear that the crucial role in this respect was played by the statist conception of socialism with which the CPY came to power, not by any objective necessity independent of that conception. It can be seen that the notions of "objective necessity" and "objective fact" are well suited to the ideological distortion of history when separated from the commitments of its principal actors.

Yugoslavia affirmed that a small country cannot create anything historically significant in this world of massive concentrations of material and military power unless it is prepared for resistance and sacrifice in order to protect its independence. That small countries are not beyond hope provided that they possess these qualities was convincingly shown by the example of the Vietnamese Revolution. And this was, among other things, the catalyst for the antiwar movement and the New Left in the West, just as Yugoslavia's example stimulated differentiation within the Eastern camp and in general among the communist parties of the world.

The concepts of authoritarian and pauperistic communism had the upper hand in the Yugoslav Revolution. It formulated its authoritarianism under the influence of Stalinism. But its pauperism harkened back to the War Communism of Lenin's Bolsheviks, for the heroic morality of the Partisans was ascetic, collectivist, and egalitarian.

The copying of the statist model after the war led to the appearance of serious symptoms of degeneration on the part of the new regime. The broad masses of the people lived ascetically, collectivistically, and in an egalitarian manner. But in the inner circles of the party-state apparatus, privilege, the high life, differentiated housing and settlement patterns, and similar phenomena began to spread.[44] In today's terms these privileges were not conspicuous. But they were most painful to see for the people, who lived in dire need.

The conflict with Stalin moved the CPY leadership to subject the authoritarian-statist conception of socialism to re-examination. Since the blockade of Yugoslavia imposed further renunciations, the pauperistic aspect of communist politics and ideology became a subject of critical inquiry only somewhat later. After the 1948 break an anti-Stalinist social bloc in Yugoslavia was gradually created. Through the end of the 1950s it appeared to be homogeneous. But then it began to become sharply differentiated, confronted with new trials and temptations and changed circumstances. Thenceforth several conflicting tendencies in Yugoslavia went under the common appellation of *self-managing socialism*. For our purposes, the most important were these three: *liberalized statism, bourgeois socialism,* and *democratic socialism.*

* * *

The party-state leadership was the first to expound and elaborate the basic ideas of the program of de-statization. These ideas were workers' and social self-management, the withering away of the state and the transcendence of politics as alienated social power, and the transformation of the Communist Party of Yugoslavia into the League of Communists in Yugoslavia. What was accomplished?

The most important legacy of de-statization was the development of self-management *at the workplace.* It was first instituted in the economy and then broadened to other areas as well. In practice, however, self-management has been limited to problems of production and distribution. Genuinely political questions are tacitly reserved for the organizations of the LCY, particularly its leadership.[45]

In the vertical organization of society there were also created a series of forms and institutions which were termed "self-managing"—assemblies of delegates from the commune, republic, and federal levels; communities of interest; and diverse associations and chambers. Since there are no *real* elections for these bodies, all this is merely *formal* self-management. Were such elections to take place, the resulting system, encompassing some two million delegates of various sorts, would be democratic almost second to none.

Self-management is the democratic component of the existing system. But it is also exploited as the ideology of the status quo. Along with genuine self-management *in work collectives*[46] there has been cultivated an ideological picture of Yugoslavia as a *"society* of workers' and social self-management." Such *summary* pronouncements about self-management are ideological. Real self-management is measured by concrete freedoms and rights, as well as by the opportunities that exist for the citizen to use them.

From the ideological pretense of a "self-managing society" the conclusion necessarily follows, by simple deduction, that every major institution and organization in that society is self-managing in character. On this logic any pressure from below to change these institutions and organizations, or even merely to subject them to fundamental criticism, can *by definition* be characterized as an attack on self-management. All this is intended to prevent the authoritarian-statist conception of the *political* system of socialism from being brought seriously into question.[47]

The slogan "Factories to the workers!" heralded, in its own time, the beginnings of de-statization in Yugoslavia. Today what should be demanded is nothing less than radical socialist democratization, which means workers' and social self-management from top to bottom. This is the major watershed between democratic socialism and liberalized statism.

There is no more urgent need than for Marxists to set to work in constructing the political theory of socialism. The founders of bourgeois democracy knew in advance that power corrupts. Consequently, they proceeded realistically from personal and group interests, attempting to bring them face to face and into equilibrium as much as possible, and to divide power. Astonishingly, many Marxists have become helpless moralists, seeking the sole guarantee against the abuse of the new power that has fallen into their hands in the personal qualities of those who exercise that power. While the former have woven variations on the Marxist theme of the withering away of the state, the latter have seized a monopoly of power in the name of Marxism. Before the state withers away, it must be lived in just the same. But the distinction between the good and the bad state has also been forgotten. Nothing of any consequence has been done to design and create defenses and counterbalances to this political monopoly. And it is not true that nothing can be done in this respect so long as only one party continues to rule.

The record to date offers no basis for the official assessment that in Yugoslavia the historical process has begun of the withering away of the state and of the transcendence of politics as alienated social power dominated by a particular professional group. After the victorious revolution the state appropriated the key resources of production and management of all areas of social life. At that time an *enormous* party-state apparatus was created. From 1950 to the present this apparatus has been considerably *decentralized* and its *competences reduced*. It is true that the role of the political-state apparatus in Yugoslavia is smaller than in any other country governed by a communist party. But by the same token it is substantially larger than in many other countries, the capitalist countries in particular.

Much effort and even more words have been invested in the process of de-statization in Yugoslavia. To grasp our situation by the root, however, means to grasp the role of the ruling party. The Yugoslavs live in a political society. In it the Party is the basic factor of rule, continuity, and change. No further democratization is possible in such a society so long as democracy in the Party is still in its infancy. Any critique of statism which sidesteps the Party concerns itself with its secondary aspect—state administration. Any attempt to approach the problem of de-statization independently of the Party testifies to the failure of the investigator to liberate himself from the Party's charismatic grasp.

In order to place themselves at a distance from other systems ruled by communist parties, our official spokesmen assert that Yugoslavia is not a one-party system (although neither, obviously, is it a multi-party system). In fact, Yugoslavia is distinguished from these countries not by virtue of its party structure, but by virtue of more liberal policies and more liberal relations within the Party, the development of self-management at the workplace, a market economy. . . .

A critical analysis of the Party must be preceded by an acknowledgment that the idea of the Party's transformation into a League of Communists accomplished nothing of substance. The numerous proclamations of radical Party reform have ended in more than modest results: reorganizations.

Not only does the Party relate to the workers as a "class in itself" incomparably more than as a "class for itself;" within the Party, too, there is in practice a division between a kind of Party for itself (the leadership) and a Party in itself (the membership). The dominant influence on its policies and on all political life in Yugoslavia is exercised by people who were educated in the spirit of the communism of the late Third International. Not even in the LCY, which according to newspaper accounts is superior to all other ruling communist parties, has intraparty democracy attained the level known in the Bolshevik Party prior to its Tenth Congress in 1921.

Those who belong to the Party are people of very heterogeneous social origins, interests, and thoughts. Other factors, too, operate against monolithism: the degree of economic development, the general level of education, the country's openness to ideological and political influences from the rest of the world, as well as differentiation within the international communist movement. Sooner or later the monolithic conception of the Party will have to be abandoned and reconciled with the diversity of its composition and of the composition of the environment in which it acts, as well as with the developmental needs of Yugoslavia. Hitherto, it has always been efforts to reconcile reality with the monolithic and centralistic principle that have predominated. Thanks to the domination of this principle, all currents and orientations in the Party have publicly adopted the same platform, but only *in the abstract.*

In the LCY there is still no attempt made to verify whether a majority of the members do, in fact, stand behind a given policy decision. In the Party true elections do not exist and virtually without exception there is one candidate for each major position. The leadership renews itself in accordance with its own taste. All really serious conflicts in the political summit are resolved within that narrow circle and never has an extraordinary Party Congress been called to deal with such questions. The public learns of these conflicts only when news of the corresponding expulsions or resignations is officially released.

What would happen if, at a future Party Congress, there were elected several leading organs which were truly independent of each other and responsible only to the Congress—say, executive, auditing, and informational? Let us leave little to the imagination: in addition to these organs, in which professional politicians must necessarily participate, the Congress might also elect a body composed of "ordinary" members who would take part in the total range of work of these organs (apart from voting) and who would set forth an independent evaluation of the state of affairs within the Party prior to the next Congress.

In the Party the right of the minority openly to advocate changes in adopted policies is not recognized. It is maintained that this would lead to Party paralysis. But this claim is unjustified, for a democratically adopted policy would be in force by mandate so long as the minority has not become a majority.

The members of Party organizations are internally divided and this makes it possible for the leading circles to exercise a monopoly of power. They are an ineluctable mediating force, since "ordinary" communists do not have the right to communicate *directly* in efforts to influence Party policies. Since the leading circles can expel members and even dissolve entire Party organizations, this means that the leadership determines their behavior in an essential way, rather than the other way around. The theoretical possibility exists that in this manner the leading circles can vitally alter the Party's composition. In the history of communism this has certainly happened on occasion.

While "ordinary" Party members are politically atomized, this is also true of workers and of citizens in general. The professional political apparatus still has the final word in the Party and in society at large. Proclamations about the deprofessionalization of politics are insufficient when the monopoly of professional politicians and qualitative differences among them are there to be seen.

If in its internal life a communist party is still largely a party typical of the Third International, then its relations with other organizations and institutions can certainly be no different. This evaluation is not affected by the fact that the Party's leading circles are no longer identical with those of the state administration or of mass political organizations in a personal sense. There is a real division of labor and jurisdiction between the Party and other organizations. But it is no less accurate to say that the other components of the system are still the Party's transmission belts. The Party is guaranteed influence in them in advance by virtue of the assignment of its disciplined cadres to *all important* posts. In these posts it is almost unheard of to find someone who is not a Party member.

The Party is not obliged to struggle for influence through argument alone. This situation is in conflict with the idea that the Party ought to act as an internal, rather than an external, vanguard. To be sure, there have been sincere attempts to exert the Party's influence primarily through force of argument, but the Party, afraid of the consequences of operating in this manner, has returned to the old method of direction whenever serious disagreements have surfaced.

* * *

We have argued that Yugoslavia is just beginning to face the prospect of a coming of age in a transition from *authoritarian* to democratic communism. On the other side of the coin, *pauperistic* communism has been abandoned in record time.

Of asceticism not so much as a trace has remained; everyone is involved in trying to achieve a high material standard of living. During and immediately after the war, collectivism held in check the aspiration for the satisfaction of individual and group interests, but "interest" was thereafter rapidly conceived as a stimulus to social progress and as an individual and group right. Serious differences in wages and incomes have long been permitted without reservation in order to stimulate productivity, creativity, and educational achievement.

But in place of the former asceticism, substantial inroads have been made by a vulgar consumerist hedonism. And at times it seems as if individual and group egoism is the sole realistic alternative to the collectivism which has since been transcended. Egalitarianism in material distribution has been rejected, but nowadays any and all principles of social equality are in constant jeopardy. Alongside of the critique of the "egalitarian syndrome," a truly antiegalitarian syndrome has developed and flourished.

Uravnilovka, of course, is unjustified both on its own merits and because it inhibits economic and social progress. But does this really also justify excessive differences between individual categories and strata of the population? What would remain of socialism were we to attempt increasingly to divide ourselves into a consumer society on the one hand, and a society of want on the other?

To say that equality is the foundation of communism assumes, according to Marx, that it is politically justified. Social equality belongs to the network of ideals of Marxist socialism; inequality does not. We are not speaking here of primitive egalitarianism, but of distribution according to work combined with guarantee of a minimum standard of living and greater equalization of opportunity for education, health care, and the cultural uplifting of each individual, regardless of his or her labor contribution.

How else are we to carry out further modernization, instead of hindering it, if we do not increase the prospects of social equality and justice as well as the participation of the broad masses in public life? How much social differentiation constitutes a truly *unavoidable* price for the deliverance from want? We will not, one hopes, be told that there is some iron law of social differentiation analogous to Michels' "iron law of oligarchy." Discussions of the stratification of Yugoslav society concern themselves as a rule with the economic side of the problem, forgetting that the existing distribution of political power is also a potent source of social differentiation.

De-statization in the economy would certainly not have been possible without the reaffirmation of the market. Even Lenin sensed that socialism would not be in any position simply to eliminate the commodity character of production. This is why he sought salvation from the economic dead-end of War Communism in the NEP. To be sure, Lenin had wanted the market confined to the sphere of small property-holders and viewed NEP as a temporary retreat from socialism. But even this was too great a sacrilege for the dogmatists among the Bolsheviks, who quickly replaced NEP with an economy that was totally centralized, distributive, and statist.

The CPY laid this dogma, too, to rest in the museum of antiquities, showing that economics in socialism must possess market characteristics. But those who construed de-statization in a bourgeois manner were not satisfied with this and began to make a fetish of *market spontaneity* as an end in itself. In Yugoslavia in the second half of the 1960s, this went so far as to generate a resurgence of the *laissez-faire* conception of the market.

The market began to be seen as a collection of mutually opposed self-managing enterprises and banks that were totally protected from broader social influence and that had legitimate interests in increasing their income on the market *at any price.* The next move was the demand to introduce market measures into all other areas, including the school system, culture, housing policy, and health care. And all of this was purportedly for the sake of the further socialization of property and the development of self-management. In reality this path was leading to *group* property and *group-particularistic* self-management. The technocratic strata firmly embraced economic liberalism because they sensed that the prospects for oligarchic groups would be very bright in self-management so conceived.

The most extreme advocates of the market sought freedom for "self-managing capital" and proposed the introduction of "self-managing stockholding." By transforming the producers into stockholders of some sort, they were to be given a greater stake in the fate of their enterprises. But what kind of a society would it be that, after a short-lived idyll of egalitarian and "self-managing" stockholding, become divided into those with shares and those without?

A true picture of the potential scope of unbridled economic liberalism was available only beyond Yugoslavia's borders. Several Yugoslav firms were registered abroad in the names of their managers, who proceeded to behave quite like proprietors; the purchasing, export, and exploitation of labor power was expanded; and there was increased pressure to eliminate all substantive controls on export and import as well as on foreign investment.

Capitalism, in historical perspective, has developed from classical, anti-statist liberalism to neoliberalism, which not only permits but demands state intervention in the economy, the bridling of market spontaneity, and attempts to resolve the mass of accumulated social problems through the "welfare state."

In Yugoslavia in the 1960s there were increasingly strong tendencies toward movement in the opposite direction: from statism to an economic liberalism with strong affinities with liberalism of the *laissez-faire* variety.

As the antithesis of the feudal state, classical liberalism played a revolutionary role throughout the world. In time, however, it became such a fetter to progress that its advocates have long since been targeted as conservatives. Contrary to classical liberalism, neoliberalism exhibits a certain similarity to statism, as well as to socialism.

In Yugoslavia economic liberalization, as the opposite of statist economics, also had a positive function. But economic liberalism quickly revealed its own dark side: the establishment of a peculiar variety of *capitalist* relationships between work collectives.

Economic liberalism necessarily created market anarchy, a new form of contradiction between the social character of production and group-private ownership, as well as unacceptable social differences. The statists, naturally, sought relief from such crises in state intervention. In turn, once the economy was smothered with accelerated state-imposed measures, the economic liberals appeared anew on the scene.

The social pendulum will swing like this between the state and market spontaneity so long as there is not constructed an all-embracing system of workers' and social self-management that would unite market competition with democratic social planning and direction. Insofar as such an economy and such a society are without historical precedent, it is understandable that it is not easy to find the right solution on the basis of our existing knowledge.

Nevertheless, liberalized statism and bourgeois socialism are not equally well rooted in the Yugoslav soil. Whenever the opportunity of directly measuring both has presented itself, the latter has proved to be the weaker. On these occasions the statists have easily taken advantage of the dissatisfaction of the broad masses with the consequences of market spontaneity and have vitally restricted the political freedom won during the process of de-statization heretofore.

* * *

It can be said without exaggeration that for Yugoslavia the past three and a half decades have represented not only an historical period, but an historical epoch. Without the Communist Party of Yugoslavia the rebirth of Yugoslavia from the ruins left by foreign occupation as well as civil and religious war would not have been possible. The revolution strongly accelerated the course of historical development in this corner of the world.

In the Yugoslav federation there is considerable autonomy and equality of the component units, nations, and national minorities. From a backward agrarian country, Yugoslavia has been transformed in these thirty-five years into an industrial-agrarian country nearly at the middle stage of development.[48] Because the CPY rejected the dogma of the forced collectivization of the countryside, Yugoslavia's agriculture has been considerably modernized. In the production of consumer goods, in terms of assortment as well as quantity, Yugoslavia hardly lags at all behind the nearly developed Western countries. Schooling, health care, and social services are accessible to the broad masses. Employee self-management is developing in work collectives. Individual areas of art, science, and philosophy have blossomed. Finally, Yugoslavia is the only open state in the world that is ruled by a communist party. And this is one of the reasons for the growth of the ambitious expectations of the population at large.

We Yugoslavs, therefore, live in a society which, according to material indicators, has very nearly approached the middle tier of developed countries. But there is also considerable political poverty in Yugoslav society. Under pressure from the progressive element of the leadership and membership, the Party's conservative wing periodically agrees to make democratic promises and declarations. But ideology always establishes attractive goals whose real and concrete meaning is revealed only in practice. "It turns out that words are not the eye of a needle, but doors that are wide open to all. One passes through them easily, as from darkness to the morning light."[49] Whether a regime is for real democratization or not is to be measured by whether it is prepared to accept the unavoidable consequences of democratization: criticism of its own work, the possibility of being replaced, the appearance of "undesirable" people in the public political arena. . . .

There will be no escape from the cycle of alternating political "relaxation" and "tightening" so long as the Party fails to transform itself from the guardian of the existing order into the initiator of the *socialist movement*. For Marx, communism was preeminently a movement. And many communists still treat "the party" as synonymous with "the movement." Yet in all socialist revolutions to the present day the militant movement was broader than the communist party alone. Only after the seizure of power has the party eliminated the movement's other participants from the political stage. How is the revolutionary and post-revolutionary dictatorship to be democratized unless communists return to the idea of a "movement"? In the socialist movement the Party would have no advance guarantees; it would have to struggle for influence through example, persuasion, and argument.

Fundamental political reform will be as elusive as a mirage so long as democratic-socialist pressure is not articulated from below. It is clear that only a political movement can draw people out of their state of practical inertia. There are plenty of people in the Party who secretly hope for the development of some sort of socialist movement, but when its first traces begin to appear many are seized with fear of innovation and risk.

This is why the student movement of 1968 was so thoroughly crushed. This was the first time that the party-state hierarchy had experienced a mass challenge from the democratic left and it was decided to smash it while it was still in the "group fusion" stage. It was asserted by some at the time that the closing off of the leftist outlet from political crises usually leads to shifts to the right. And how else to explain the extent of the breakthrough of the nationalist right two years later?

The real question is not, "Why should the working class *as a class* be enabled to enter onto the political stage?" but rather, "In whose real interest is it?" In Yugoslavia the Party, by forcing the pace of industrialization, has merely created the conditions for the rapid development of the working class. But what was created in this process was a working class — fragmented — that corresponded to the Party's political monopoly. How can the working populace truly become a class for itself unless it does not organize and engage itself, particularly in politics? The point is precisely that it is not enough to have a workers' ideology; what is needed is a workers' politics. But the best guarantee of a workers' politics is mass participation by the workers in political decision-making at all levels.

The inadequate developmental level and lack of education of the working people can no longer be used to justify the state of affairs in Yugoslavia. We have long had mighty industrial centers, yet the working people's participation in their political life has been minimal. And as far as education is concerned, Yugoslav workers on the average have now attained a higher educational level than the bourgeoisie when it became the ruling class, not only within Yugoslavia's boundaries but in the West as well.

It is to be hoped that the democratic current within the Party will finally become strong enough vis-à-vis the guardians of past and present that it will come to rely on pressure from below and commit itself to the creation of a socialist movement. This will not happen easily or quickly. And how could it, when the goal is a radical transformation? The preservation of a minimum of stability is only one of the things about which a small country situated between the two global blocs need be concerned. All the intelligent and progressive forces of the people must gather together to conceptualize and put into effect a realistic program of socialist democratization. Yugoslavia, of all the countries ruled by communist parties, has the greatest prospects in this regard.

7. The Challenge of Democratic Communism

In the democratic capitalist states there is another great movement which is undergoing vital changes. Democratic communism ("Eurocommunism") differs from authoritarian communism no less than, say, contemporary liberalism from classical liberalism or reformist social democracy from revolutionary socialism.

Both democratic capitalism and authoritarian communism have found in the new communism a powerful critic that cannot persuasively be accused of either anti-democratic motives on the one hand, or of anti-communism on the other.

Capitalism is still in a position to legitimize itself relative to (authoritarian) communism on two grounds. The first is democracy. Authoritarian communism has succeeded in capitalist (and other) dictatorships, not in capitalist democracies. The masses who enjoy a variety of freedoms in capitalism—the freedom to associate into political parties and trade unions, to strike and to demonstrate, to select their employers, to bargain over wages and work conditions, to travel—do not desire social changes that would cause them to lose these privileges. The second relative advantage of democratic capitalism is founded on the ability of highly developed capitalism to enable the population to enjoy an enviable standard of living, in which one cannot fail to include a rather high level of social security. To be sure, this latter achievement must be credited more to the social democratic parties than to the capitalistically oriented ones.

Today, capitalism is confronted with a new communism, one that is appropriate with respect to both *ends* and *means*. Democratic socialism as a goal is best served by democratic political means. But, again, a firm commitment to such means must sooner or later lead to the rejection of violent revolution and the "dictatorship of the proletariat." The most influential communist parties in the West have concluded that such a revolution is neither likely, necessary, nor even desirable. For the manner in which a party governs society depends not so much on its good will and ultimate goals as on the nature of the path by which it comes to power. He who appropriates power by force will guard it by means of dictatorship.

Dogmatists among anti-communists and communists alike reject the term "democratic communism." The following quotation from William Safire will serve to illustrate the position of the former: "Since Communists have adopted democratic means, some leftists think Communists have adopted democratic goals. This is a dangerous delusion. . . . *A non-totalitarian form of Communism is a contradiction in terms.*"[50]

In seeking guarantees from the new communism in the West, the greatest fuss is usually raised by those who have no right to do so since they have always applied a double standard—more lenient for rightist dictatorships and more severe for those of the left. Among them are individuals who have approved or at least failed to condemn the assaults of rightist states against democratic leftist governments.

In the view of the dogmatic anti-communists, Western communists have merely altered their tactics in order to lull and delude the defenders of democracy. These dogmatists still adhere to the primitive understanding of ideology as a collection of lies.

More sophisticated skeptics do not question the sincerity of changes in the political means and the ideology of the Western communist parties, but they doubt that these changes have affected the communists' innermost temperament. If the communist parties come to power, it is argued, their proclivities toward authoritarianism and coercive rule will become manifest. Here, ideology is seen as self-delusion rather than a collection of lies. So long as the communist parties exploited democratic mechanisms without altering their ideology, the skeptics insisted that their long-range ideological goals were still of primary importance. But now, when the ideological arsenal of these parties has been subjected to fundamental critical revision, the skeptics suddenly bring to bear a rather different notion of ideology. It turns out that ideology does not affect basic inclinations and commitments. The Stalinists have a far better understanding of the role of ideology in communist parties, sounding the alarm on anyone who hints that it be changed.

For the communist dogmatists "authoritarian communism" is a contradiction in terms, while "democratic communism" is a superfluous concept since all communism is democratic *by definition*. In reality, they are intimately convinced that those communist parties which have rejected armed revolution, the "dictatorship of the proletariat," and a one-party order are no longer communist parties at all and are instead on the path to undergoing a social-democratic metamorphosis and becoming integrated into the capitalist system.

In world communism a process is unfolding which, in its deepest implications, can be compared only with the split between the Third and Second Internationals. Not a single conflict within communism to this day has been of such ideological scope, for until now changes in the basic ideological core have not been at issue. It is as if the Second International were now repaying the Third in kind! Authoritarian communism introduced a series of prejudices and even myths in the assessment of social democracy, both before the First World War and later. Because of this, several standard histories of Marxism and the workers' movement are in need of serious revision. This does not mean that we should forget that a good part of social democracy behaved nationalistically during the First World War and the period of decolonization, nor that we should relate any less critically to capitalism.

If communists in power sincerely wish to support the new communism, they themselves will have to submit to democratization. The manner in which a communist evaluates democracy in the capitalist countries is a rather precise indicator of whether he maintains a democratic or authoritarian vision of socialism. The Stalinist gives himself away through his *a priori* identification of formal democracy with capitalism and real democracy with socialism ("real" socialism, of course). Ideologies often transform empirical questions into transcendental ones.

In *ideologized* Marxism there is total confusion between Marx's concepts of class *rule* and class *dictatorship*—and, indeed, Marx himself at times was careless in using these terms interchangeably. The authoritarian communists had reached the ideological conclusion that any manner of capitalist rule is *more or less* equivalent to capitalist dictatorship. Subsequently the Stalinists shifted the emphasis from "less" to "more," and finally they eliminated even that reservation. Thus they were incapable of distinguishing between democratic and dictatorial capitalism — and this, we may well suppose, had catastrophic political consequences in the 1930s throughout the world.

Nor are Stalinists in any position to register the important distinction between *capitalist democracy* and *democracy in capitalism*. It is difficult to deny that democracy is heavily laden with universal human content, that it stands in a relationship of continuity with the bourgeois-democratic revolutions, and that it is also in large part the result of the long and hard struggle of the working class and its parties for the democratization of capitalism. The communist who sneers at this democracy is in the final analysis denigrating the efforts and achievements of those social forces with which he ostensibly professes solidarity. It is laughable to assert that this is merely formal democracy when there freely operate within it anti-capitalist parties which even have a prospect of coming to power via the parliamentary path.

It is one thing when Western democracy is criticized by the proponents of statist dictatorship, but it is quite another when this is done by a communist who is attempting to subject capitalism to radical democratic-socialist reform. Not only has statism failed to surpass the level of democracy in capitalism; it has not yet even attained it. By looking down their noses at this democracy, the statists only weakly conceal their own feelings of inferiority.

It is indeed distinctive of Marxism that it should point to the contrast between the formal and substantive dimensions of democracy in class society. This contrast arises as a result of the differences between *legal equality* and *equality,* between the rights of the citizen and the opportunity to utilize them. It is strikingly anticipated in Herbert Marcuse's ostensibly paradoxical concept of "repressive tolerance." From this, however, it does not at all follow that democratic forms in capitalism are bereft of any serious content. Nothing is easier than to verify whether the Stalinist intimately believes the contrary to be true. Not a single one is on record who would *dare* allow in his domain, for example, anything on the order of Hyde Park Corner, however scornfully he may speak of it.

The Stalinists' complex toward "formal democracy" is also manifested in the manner in which they always imitate its forms once they have been carefully emptied of all content. Thus they hold pre-election campaigns even though there is only one candidate for each position; and the Stalinist triumphantly contrasts the apathy of electorates in the capitalist countries with the participation of nearly all voters in his own.

Thanks to the private ownership of the means of production and managerial administration, practically no democracy exists in the capitalist economy and at the workplace in general. Under these conditions democracy is more a matter of participation in a periodical political game than a concern of everyday life. "For the absolute boundary of bourgeois representative democracy lies in the fundamental contradiction which is contained in the chronic undermining of its basic rights: in those places where people obtain experience and have concrete knowledge about social processes, in the spheres where they immediately work and live, public accessibility and self-government are reduced to a minimum; however, where they are left to secondary information, where they are degraded to observers of the marketplace of ideas, people play the role of free citizens capable of making decisions."[51]

The indisputable truth that political democracy is not a *sufficient condition* for complete democracy is interpreted by the Stalinist ideologists, however, as if it were also not a *necessary condition* for democracy! Some of what are otherwise universal rights, such as the freedom to travel, to choose one's residence, the right to information, and so forth, are made in statism into privileges for small circles of individuals. To be sure, the occasional Stalinist in power will acknowledge in confidence that there is indeed no political democracy in his country, but he will immediately add that this is compensated by the existence of economic democracy. But this is an ideological myth. Because the state in such societies has a monopoly on economic power, it is difficult to see how economic democracy could be possible without political democracy. In these countries there is no economic democracy even within the enterprise, for the workers do not participate in management even as much as they do in capitalist enterprises.

According to Joseph Schumpeter it was once anticipated that the democratic method would be "that institutional arrangement for arriving at political decisions which realizes the common good by *making the people itself decide issues through the election of individuals who are to assemble in order to carry out its will.*"[52] In real life, however, the democratic method has turned out to be "that institutional arrangement for arriving at political decisions in which *individuals acquire the power to decide by means of a competitive struggle for the people's vote.*"[53] Thus is the path traversed from the rule of the people to the reality of the rule of parties—to "democracy without the people," in the expression of Maurice Duverger.

But the weaknesses of the multiparty arrangement are only brought to an extreme rather than eliminated in the one-party system. Here the "democratic" method is that institutional arrangement for arriving at political decisions in which individuals "assert" their power (either achieved by force or inherited from their superiors) by means of a noncompetitive "struggle" for the people's vote. Of course, it is not to be expected that a party holding a power monopoly will allow onto the political stage those groups which at one time both drove it into illegality and which were its adversaries in civil war and revolution. A pluralistic political system in the post-revolutionary dictatorship can sooner arise through the spontaneous division of the ruling party, and moreover only on the condition that the balance of power does not permit either opposing faction to eliminate the others from the political scene.

Democratic socialism attempts to reestablish and simultaneously radicalize the classical concept of democracy as the rule of the people. *Popular self-government* ought to be introduced into *all areas* of social life and made as *substantive* and *direct* as possible. In the absence of this there is no socialism. The slogan of different paths to socialism cannot conceal the existence of essentially different conceptions of socialism — democratic and authoritarian.

NOTES TO PART TWO

1. See the section on "Private Property and Communism" in the "Economic and Philosophical Manuscripts of 1844," in *The Marx-Engels Reader,* pp. 81 ff.
2. "The German Ideology," in *The Marx-Engels Reader,* p. 161.
3. Great Britain, the USA, and Holland. Engels added France and Germany.
4. This is what Lenin wrote in his "Contribution to the History of the Question of the Dictatorship" in 1920:

    "The question of the dictatorship of the proletariat is the fundamental question of the modern working-class movement in all capitalist countries without exception."

    "One cannot be a revolutionary *in fact* unless one prepares for dictatorship."

    "Major questions in the life of nations are resolved only by force."

    See V. I. Lenin, *Collected Works* (Moscow: Progress, 1966), Vol. 31, pp. 340, 344, 346.
5. C. Wright Mills, *The Marxists* (New York: Dell, 1962), p. 29.
6. Peter Berger, *Pyramids of Sacrifice* (New York: Basic Books, 1974).
7. Interview with Jean-Paul Sartre, as cited in *The New York Review of Books,* March 26, 1970.
8. The term "spaceship earth" was coined by Kenneth Boulding; "stationary equilibrium" by Robert Heilbroner.
9. Wolfgang Harich, *Kommunismus ohne Wachstum.*
10. Leon Trotsky, *The Russian Revolution,* trans. Max Eastman (New York: Doubleday, 1959), p. 483.
11. V. I. Lenin, "The Proletarian Revolution and the Renegade Kautsky," in *The Lenin Anthology,* ed. Robert C. Tucker (New York: Norton, 1975), p. 466.
12. Berger, p. 77.
13. The servants were also killed.
14. Fyodor Dostoyevsky, *The Brothers Karamazov,* trans. Constance Garnett (New York: Random House, 1950), pp. 287, 291.
15. Max Weber, "Politics as a Vocation," in *From Max Weber: Essays in Sociology,* trans. and ed. H. H. Gerth and C. Wright Mills (New York: Oxford University Press, 1946), p. 125.
16. Marx, "Economic and Philosophical Manuscripts of 1844," in *The Marx-Engels Reader,* pp. 68–69.
17. Yevgeniy Zamyatin, *My* (We).
18. J. Andzejeuski (Andrzejewski), *Tama pokriva zemlju* [Darkness Covers the Earth] (Sarajevo, 1963), p. 64.
19. By analogy with the terms oligarch/y, monarch/y, etc. I have coined the terms charismarch (xápioma + apxos) and charismarchy.
20. At the same time he decisively rejects any true minority in the party which would advocate changing the party line.
21. Mao Tse-tung remarked, "Probably Mr. Khrushchev fell because he had no cult of personality

at all." From an interview given to Edgar Snow on January 9, 1965; see Edgar Snow, *The Long Revolution* (New York: Random House, 1972), p. 205.

22. Niccolo Machiavelli, *The Prince,* trans. Thomas G. Bergin (New York: Appleton-Century-Crofts, 1947), p. 29.

23. Sartre, *Search for a Method,* p. 107.

24. Dobrica Ćosić, *Vreme smrti* [A Time of Death] (Belgrade, 1975), Vol. III, p. 186.

25. Albert Camus, *The Rebel.*

26. Cited in Boris Souvarine, *Stalin* (New York: Alliance, 1939), p. 317.

27. Cited in Alexander Barmine, *One Who Survived* (New York: Putnam, 1945), p. 94.

28. ". . . absolute and strict *unity of will,* which directs the joint labours of hundreds, thousands, and tens of thousands of people. The technical, economic, and historical necessity of this is obvious and all those who have thought about socialism have always regarded it as one of the conditions of socialism. But how can strict unity of will be ensured? By thousands subordinating their will to the will of one." Lenin, "The Immediate Tasks of the Soviet Government," in *The Lenin Anthology,* p. 455.

29. Naturally, this does not mean that there is a sharp boundary between them.

30. Roy Medvedev cites data illustrating the growth of vast social differences and contrasting them to the Bolsheviks' initial egalitarianism. See his *On Socialist Democracy* (New York: Knopf, 1975).

31. Ovid in the *Metamorphoses.*

32. See Eugene Kamenka, *Marxism and Ethics* (New York: Macmillan, 1969), p. 60.

33. Yevgeniy Zamyatin, "On Literature, Revolution, and Entropy," 1923; cited from the anthology *Sever* (Belgrade, 1963), p. 27.

34. See the text of Ernst Bloch's speech to the opening session of the 1968 Korčula Summer School, published in *Praxis,* No. 1–2/1969. [Translator's Note: The Korčula Summer School was an annual international event between 1964 and 1973, organized by the members of the *Praxis* Editorial Board.]

35. Adrian Hsia speaks of "the natural proclivity of the Chinese to project their utopian visions into the past rather than the future." See his *The Chinese Cultural Revolution,* trans. Gerald Onn (New York: McGraw-Hill, 1972), p. 97.

36. Mao Tse-tung: "The ancients said, 'The principle of Kings Wen and Wu was to alternate tension with relaxation.' [Confucius, *Book of Rites*]. If a bowstring is too taut it will snap." Edgar Snow, *The Other Side of the River: Red China Today* (New York: Random House, 1961), p. 114.

37. Oscar Wilde, "The Soul of Man Under Socialism," in *The Essays of Oscar Wilde* (New York: Cosmopolitan Books, 1916), pp. 19–20.

38. Snow, *The Long Revolution,* p. 175 (my emphasis—S.S.). This is in obvious contrast to Mao's *optimism and hedonistic communism* of 1949: "We believe that revolution can change everything and that before long there will arise a new China with a big population and a great wealth of products, where life will be abundant and culture flourish." See "The Bankruptcy of the Idealistic Conception of History," cited in James Hsiung, *Ideology and Practice: The Evolution of Chinese Communism* (New York: Praeger, 1970), p. 78.

39. There is not even a hint of it in, for example, the Survey History of the League of Communists of Yugoslavia *(Pregled istorije Saveza komunista Jugoslavije),* which was prepared and published in 1963 by a group of authors at the direction of the LCY and with its approval. [Translator's Note: In 1952 the Communist Party of Yugoslavia (CPY) was redesignated the League of Communists of Yugoslavia (LCY) at the Sixth Party Congress. In this text the author variously uses the abbreviations "CPY" and "LCY" depending upon the historical period (pre- or post-1952) under discussion, while the informal shorthand of "the Party" is used throughout. The translation follows the author's usage.]

40. Official spokesmen assert that these attacks were necessary for the Party to be able to anticipate the difficult times of the war against Nazism in a spirit of unity. But this is nothing

more than conjurings of the proponents of monolithism, for there is no necessary psychological connection, not to mention a logical one, between the level of preparedness for the common struggle against Nazism and acceptance of the canons of socialist realism and dialectical-historical materialism. It was the latter which was the issue at the time.

41. Once when the proletarian units were formed, and a second time when the Second Session of AVNOJ [the Antifascist Council for the National Liberation of Yugoslavia—Trans.] of November 29-30, 1943, formed a provisional government.

42. To cite a dialogue conducted in the highest council of the leadership:

"'There is grain, only you will not go about seizing it very aggressively,' reacted Kidrić. 'You don't want to alienate the kulaks. That is pure opportunism on your part.'

"A painful silence descended. Veselinov tried to take the floor, but the words stuck in his throat. His eyes full of tears, he barely uttered: 'No, it's not opportunism! It's the simple truth that there is no grain, yet we want the peasants to create it out of thin air. So we have literally gone to war with them. Thousands of peasants have been arrested and convicted. Some have died, too! People are defending what little grain they have grown with their hatchets. There are kulaks here too, but these are mainly our people! In the war of national liberation they were on our side, and now they have become enemies! Not because they are kulaks, but because the procurement was set too high. Our activists in charge of the procurement have set themselves apart from the people. These are the same people who were the most popular during the war, and now they have become the most despised. I think that this should not have been allowed to happen.'" Svetozar Vukmanović-Tempo, *Revolucija koja teče. Memoari* [The Revolution That Flows: Memoirs], Vol. 2, pp. 127 ff.

43. "At the meeting of the inner leadership, Blagoje Nesković, Mosa Pijade, and I were entrusted with the preparation of a draft Party statute to be presented to the Fifth Congress. We completed this assignment quickly because at our very first meeting we agreed that we would adopt the statutes of the CPSU(b) [Translator's Note: Communist Party of the Soviet Union (Bolsheviks). The parenthetical designation "(b)" was used throughout the Stalin years until it was dropped in 1952.] and that we would merely adapt them to our conditions. This was in line with our position of creating the same kind of socialism as existed in the Soviet Union and the same kind of Party as the Bolshevik Party" (*Ibid.,* p. 93).

44. "The highest state and party leading cadres were treated especially favorably. They were provided with industrial goods from 'diplomatic shops' that were intended for the use of diplomatic missions. These shops were organized on the model used in the Soviet Union. Their existence was justified by the need of the leading cadres to be free of concern for their daily requirements so that they could devote themselves to the organization of the new society. Those of us in the innermost circle of the party leadership were supplied with foodstuffs from a special store. We paid a flat rate of 1,000 dinars monthly for each member of our household and took from the store whatever we needed. *We established a peculiar sort of communism.* From the first days there appeared serious abuses in this supply system: there were individual leading personages who bought various fabrics, bed linens, and other goods in quantities far in excess of their needs; these goods were distributed to their relatives, friends. . . We had to react to these phenomena: we made a decision that only certain quantities could be bought in these stores for each household member. This reduced the level of speculation, but did not eliminate it" (*ibid.,* p. 22; my emphasis—S.S.).

"At the same time as communists were being transferred from production into administration, the material privileges associated with administrative work grew accordingly. Each ministry, general bureau and head office at the federation and republic levels, and each head office of enterprises, districts, and communal people's councils had its own economy from which it was supplied with foodstuffs at decreased prices. In addition there were villas and rest homes on the coast or in the mountains; this is where the administration summered. Communists were doubly privileged: they were shifted into administrative work and there they enjoyed significant material privileges (*ibid.,* p. 134).

45. Whenever employees—for instance at universities, in schools, the press, publishing houses, cultural institutions—tried to go beyond these boundaries, their autonomy was so much further restricted that it was no longer sensible to speak of self-management, but only of participation in management. And through the introduction of "moral-political fitness" as a legal precondition for all the more important positions it has been made possible to eliminate, if necessary, all political undesirables from them. [Translator's Note: In November 1974 the Serbian Parliament passed a law allowing the Parliament itself to order the expulsion of university professors from their positions if it found their activities to threaten "social interests;" such activity had been equally vaguely defined in the criteria of "moral-political fitness" adopted by the University of Belgrade two years earlier under intense Party pressure but which the University itself was reluctant or unable to enforce. The November 1974 law, which violated a long-standing tradition of university autonomy substantially predating the communist regime, directly resulted in the suspension of the author and seven of his colleagues from the Philosophy Faculty of the University of Belgrade in January 1975 and was in fact expressly conceived with this end in mind. See Sher, *Praxis,* pp. 226-232.]

46. This, of course, does not mean that there are no differences between formal and real self-management at this level.

47. In Slovenia a few years ago a group of 25 communist deputies was sharply attacked and suppressed when they sought to add one more name at their own initiative to the official slate of candidates for the Presidency of the SFRY. [Translator's Note: SFRY = Socialist Federal Republic of Yugoslavia. The Presidency is a council of representatives from each republic and province with a rotating chairmanship. With the passing of Tito, the Chairman of the Presidency is the President of the Republic.] It did not matter that the individual they proposed was also a high and trustworthy political functionary, nor that their action was totally consistent with a law earlier passed by the Slovenian Parliament. Despite all this their action was assessed as a violation of the principle of self-management in politics!

48. The reader will find statistics to substantiate this assertion in *Jugoslavija trideset godina posle oslobedjenja i pobede nad fašizmom 1941-1975* [Yugoslavia Thirty Years After the Liberation and Triumph Over Fascism, 1941-1975] (Belgrade: Savezni zavod za statistiku, 1975).

49. Andrzejewski, p. 19.

50. William Safire, "The End of NATO?" *New York Times,* March 22, 1976; my emphasis—S.S.

51. Oskar Negt, "There is No Democracy Without Socialism, and No Socialism Without Democracy," *Das Argument,* 98, July-August 1976.

52. Joseph A. Schumpeter, *Capitalism, Socialism and Democracy,* 3rd ed. (New York: Harper & Row, 1950), p. 250; my emphasis—S.S.

53. *Ibid.,* p. 269; my emphasis—S.S.

Part Three

On the Destruction of Communist Dignity and on the Ethics of the Revolutionary

1. Why This Topic?

Ernst Bloch often returned to his favorite theme of human dignity. But even he did not treat one particular theme of this cycle—the dignity of the communist.

Communist revolutionaries have always embraced the imperative of behaving with dignity in the face of the enemy. For them the sole problem is one of practical temperament: will the revolutionary find the physical strength to act defiantly in the hands of counterrevolutionary terror? Here is a moving example of how the "steel was tempered" for this "passage of torture": "I remember . . . that someone told us Young Communists of Kruševac that imprisoned Chinese revolutionaries, in the face of the traps of the class enemy, when they had no more life to lead, stopped breathing in an act of tremendous will power and thus suffocated to death. I do not know if this was either accurate or possible—but we would practice this Chinese exercise on the Bagdala and fall unconscious on the slopes of the Kruševac hillside."[1]

Here, however, we are concerned with something else—the communist's behavior toward his own party, especially the Stalinist party. For Marxists this relationship, with respect to the question of dignity, has remained beyond the field of vision. In examining it we will attempt to take up some of the key problems of revolutionary ethics.

Under the influence of Stalinism, there developed with time a spirit of *unlimited party-mindedness* in the communist parties. The communist was prepared to subordinate everything of an individual character—interests, rights, opinions, and actions—consciously and completely to collective party activity. He was expected to forget his own individuality. The principle of absolute party-mindedness was most pregnantly expressed by the super-Stalinist Lazar Kaganovich when he stated, on one occasion, that the Bolshevik "must be . . . ready to sacrifice not only his life but his self-respect and sensitivity."[2] In this atmosphere the ideal of permanent revolution was smothered in the permanent degradation of people, in Stalin's words, of a "particular cast."

Discussions on the continuity or discontinuity between Leninism and Stalinism most frequently end in an impasse because they remain overly confined to global definitions and assessments. Only when this question is sufficiently broken down is it possible to demonstrate persuasively that there are important continuities, but no less essential discontinuities as well, between them. The critics of Stalinism who facilely and without differentiation trace its continuity with Leninism become the victims of a distorted history of Bolshevism which represents one of the Stalinists' principal ideological weapons.

One of the proofs of discontinuity lies in the fact that Lenin never expected, much less demanded, of the Bolsheviks that they sacrifice their personal dignity to the party. The practice of extracting humiliating self-criticisms and recantations began only after his death. It appears that the precedent was set by Zinoviev, Kamenev, Trotsky, Piatakov, Sokolnikov, and Yevdokimov in their *Pravda* statement of October 17, 1926. Thus dawned the age of the public humiliation and self-abasement of communists in the Stalinist party, which for endless numbers of them would ultimately lead to physical death as well.

Since Stalin's party rapidly became the *"historical a priori"* for other communist parties, the principle of unconditional party-mindedness also applied to the conduct of these parties to the Stalinist fountainhead—the Party above parties. This was super-party-mindedness. The leadership of the Yugoslav Communist Party carried out an act of world-historical importance when, in 1948, it successfully resisted Stalin's attempt to bring it to its knees.

It is not difficult to show that the critical analysis of Stalinist party-mindedness even today is of practical, as well as historical, significance. Therefore my usage of verbal tenses will deliberately vary from past to present. There follow two illustrations which are deliberately not taken from the country in which Stalinism arose.

We were reminded that fearful outcries about Stalinism are not in themselves any sort of guarantee against the repetition of history by the public recantation of the Cuban poet Herberto Padilla in 1971:

> I am moved by a sincere desire to compensate the Revolution for the harm I
> may have occasioned and to compensate myself spiritually. I may prevent

others from losing themselves stupidly. . . . Striving to look like an intellectual who was an expert in problems I had no information neither knew anything about, and following this course I committed grave faults against the true intellectual's moral code, and what is worse, against the Revolution itself.[3]

In the Chinese Communist Party, even more than in Cuba, there have been periodic campaigns of humiliation and self-abasement in the name of selfless loyalty to the revolutionary cause. Here is the statement made by Academy of Sciences President Kuo Mo-jo in 1972:

Everything that I had taught and published for forty years has been permeated with idealism. . . . Previously I helped the bourgeoisie, setting forth an idealistic philosophy. In this I committed a great error with respect to the revolutionary theory of the proletariat. I failed to live up to the expectations of the party that had saved me. In past years, while the students were trying to study the works of Marx, Engels, and Lenin, I forced them to analyze . . . Mach and my idealistic theory. . . .[4]

2. Self-Abasement in the Guise of Revolutionary Selflessness

The revolutionary's dignity is active, rather than contemplative, in character. It is not the revolutionary's lot to cultivate his personal dignity as a purely internal experience. Being totally committed to revolt against the life and society of man deprived of dignity, the communist revolutionary is an especially dignified individual. And when confronted by his own organization he must make a choice: either proudly to defy the attempt to break his resistance or to commit moral suicide by admitting his "guilt" and recanting.

When the Stalinized communist abases himself before his own party he must find some sort of ideological justification for doing so, lest he break down under the burden of self-contempt. And a rationalization is close at hand. He has already heard, in similar circumstances, that the sentiment that prevents communists from giving in *to their own party,* rather than being a source of strength, is really a survival of the "petit-bourgeois" weakness of vanity. In one of the Moscow trials, Krestinsky alluded to precisely this "defect" when pressed to explain why he had denied his guilt on the previous day. It is characteristic that the Stalinist party's leadership, which simply bubbles with self-love and conceit, is most active in attacking individual vanity. Yevgeniy Zamyatin lucidly forsaw this Stalinist path of development: "In the ancient world, this was understood by the Christians, our sole (although quite imperfect) predecessors: humility is a virtue and arrogance a vice, and that the 'We' is of God while the 'I' is of the devil."[5]

The Stalinized communist's self-abasement is interpreted not even as a necessary evil, but as the revolutionary's consummate act of selflessness. The

Stalinized communist is unprepared, after all, for dignified confrontation with his own comrades. He has invested all his resources in fostering and cultivating a readiness to act heroically in the hands of the enemy and he lacks the additional strength to stand up to his own party. In principle, good conduct toward the class enemy is distinguished by defiance, while good conduct toward the party is distinguished by self-criticism.

Intellectuals have been among the most vulnerable, for many of them have given in to the pressure of feelings of guilt over their non-proletarian origins — that peculiar version of original sin — and hope at all costs to prove their loyalty to "the proletarian cause" by distinguishing themselves, so to say *a priori,* through their unreserved faithfulness to the party. The strong anti-intellectualism evident in Stalinist parties, whose protagonists have often themselves been intellectuals, would be difficult to understand without this mechanism of self-punishment. And when they joined the party many intellectuals, by virtue of this mentality, remained permanently at the stage of candidate membership. This motif was forcefully developed by Sartre in the person of Hugo in "Dirty Hands." Since Sartre's exposition is rather well-known, I shall cite another author:

> I came to be horrified by these statements and feared that in the guise of a joke they revealed something perhaps very important about myself, namely, that I had never become totally used to the Party, that I had never been a true proletarian revolutionary, and that instead I had "attached" myself to the revolutionaries by a *mere* (!) decision (we did not feel the proletarian revolutionary spirit, in other words, as a matter — so to speak — of decision but as one of substance; either one is a revolutionary and unites with the movement into a single common body, thinks with its head and feels with its heart, or one is not, and then one is left with nothing but to *wish* to be one; in this event, however, one feels permanent guilt over not being one; guilt over being separate, different, over not having merged with the Party). When today I recall my position at that time, I am struck by the analogy of the immeasurable power of Christianity, which suggests to the believer his basic and permanent guilt; and I stood (we all did) face to face with the revolution and its party with a permanently bowed head, so that I gradually came to terms with the fact that my statements, although conceived as jokes, nevertheless represented an offense, and through thoughts such as these my self-critical faculties began to leave me.[6]

There were, of course, also intellectuals who in time succeeded in coming to their senses and in rooting out this feeling of guilt. Instead of being ashamed of their origins, they took pride in the fact that through personal commitment they had succeeded in overcoming a social determinism which drew them in a non-revolutionary or even counterrevolutionary direction. Such individuals did not suffer from feelings of inferiority toward communists of proletarian origin, for they knew that for the latter far less effort was required since their social position had already pointed them to the side of the revolution.

3. Ideology and Truth

In studies of Stalinism a great deal of attention has been devoted to its concept of the Party and of the Enemy. But those studies will remain inadequate so long as the functions of two mediating ideas go untreated, namely, the Stalinist understanding of the *objective meaning* of actions and of *objective responsibility* for them. Great ideologies—and Stalinism is undoubtedly one—have great powers of (self-) deception. Without these two connecting ideas the Stalinist mentality cannot be successfully explained.

It is not sufficient for such a communist to overcome his sense of dignity as an "instinct" of moral conduct in order to confess his "guilt" before the Party. He is also required to come to the conclusion that *in a certain sense* he was truly to blame. This, of course, is impossible if what is ascribed to him is something having no relation whatsoever to his actions. It is necessary, moreover, to distinguish between "objective" and "subjective" guilt. In the first phase of Stalinization he is not called upon to confess that he deliberately (subjectively) inflicted harm on the revolutionary cause and aided the enemy. By making such a confession he would be denying his own elementary communist integrity and would be left with suicide as the only honorable solution. Nor would the Stalinizing party gain much from such an act of expiation. It needs people who atone for their "sins" through merciless self-criticism and absolute discipline.

The countless confessions of uncommitted (mal)feasances and "subjective crimes" in late Stalinism holds nothing of interest for the study of ideology. These were physically coerced capitulations. Their massive number is an insoluble mystery only for those who fail to understand that heroes, like "saints," are rare exceptions. The real problem, indeed, is that so many people believe those confessions.

Like every man of action, the communist assumes responsibility from the outset, whether he wishes to or not, for the unintended as well as the intended consequences of his activities. Whoever desires to influence the course of society and history has greater need than others to come to terms with the difference between the subjective and objective meanings of his acts and to be prepared to take the personal consequences of each. Subjective meaning and responsibility are subordinate to the actor's intentions, while objective meaning and responsibility flow from this framework. The most difficult question, of course, is how far and on what basis?

It is solely this question that points to the existence of a broad gray area which is, in turn, the most fertile for the generation and operation of ideological consciousness. In my view, ideology is distorted consciousness. This, of course, is not a complete definition, for there are forms of distorted consciousness which surely are not ideological in character.

Ideology is not merely a pack of untruths, much less of lies. If it were, the intellectual attraction of individual ideologies would remain inexplicable and it is beyond doubt that they possess this kind of power in addition to their emotive force. It is well known that there are intelligent followers, as well as stupid ones, who believe in the truthfulness of a given ideology. In an ideology's domain the presence of distortion and its indetectability are of equal importance.

Such powers of deception and self-deception cannot be generated exclusively by interests, positions, and feelings. In influential ideologies, truth and untruth are interwoven, interpenetrated, and in a peculiar manner mutually transformed at an earlier stage. Truth is distorted while untruth is made to appear as truth. Nor do ideologies merely stay put in a cognitive sense. The ideological picture of reality often contains a truthlike premise. This is why the line of criticism which attempts to immobilize ideology by pointing *directly* to its untruthfulness is most often naive. The reason lies not only in the rootedness of ideology in the actual-voluntary sphere of human existence, but also in its (partially) truthlike basis. Therefore criticism must first affirm to what extent and in what sense an ideology is truthful. Only then will the critic be in a position to point to the specific combination and discrepancy of truth and untruth as one of the properties of ideological consciousness.

The character of any ideology depends upon which elements of a given conceptual framework are true and which untrue, and in what sense. All ideologies can be ranked on a continuum beginning with totally cognitive content and claims and ending with intellectual constructs whose potential is primarily practical.

Because of its "Marxist" origins Stalinism is an ideology with a great deal of reflective material and great intellectual ambitions. This is why Stalinists insist so strongly on ideological *education*. As a superideological phenomenon Stalinism is without peer: it presents itself as a scientific ideology and all other ideologies as unscientific. Some critics seem to take the Stalinist ideologists at their word and speak of the latters' "scientism" and "positivism." While it is accurate to say that there are elements of scientism and positivism in Stalinism's *self-concept,* it is also no less accurate that Stalinist "science" has never been able to withstand even the most elementary positivistic analyses and criteria. Only in this way is it possible to explain the great intellectual success of a type of "neopositivistic Marxism" in coming to terms with Stalinist ideology.

It must also be said that Stalinism is not very powerful in terms of generating new ideas. It arose more as a modification of the classical Marxist and especially Leninist picture of the world than as a product of its own ideas. Those who fail to observe that substantive changes are concealed behind verbal similarities will find a greater degree of continuity than really exists between classical Marxism, Leninism, and Stalinism. In fact we are dealing with a Marxism that had been Leninized, and the latter in turn Stalinized. This process has been marked by ideological distortion of many sorts.

With the Stalinists even Marx's critique of ideology achieves an ideological character. Marx first tried to show that a specific view of the world was truly *distorted* and only then asked *why,* finding the explanation in the particular position and interests of corresponding groups in the social division of labor. It is mistaken to think, as some do, that the Stalinists simply changed the order of play in such a way that the social root of ideas assumes first place while the question of their truthfulness becomes subordinate. Concerned to discredit the ideas of others at all costs, the Stalinists do not actually inquire whether they are true at all. They maintain that the specific social origin of a set of ideas in and of itself implies their untruthfulness—the "genetic error." Worse, the social origin of an idea is defined *a priori* instead of being examined. Ideas that differ from Stalinist ones are of undesirable social origin *by definition.* Thus from a *transcendental* linkage between individual social groups and their progressive or regressive nature is deduced the truthfulness or untruthfulness of their world view. For true Marxism the matter is precisely the other way around: the degree of concern for truth as a social value represents an *empirical* measure of the progressiveness of social groups.

Progressive ideologies are distinguished from conservative ones not—as the Stalinists think—by the *complete* absence of "distortedness," but by the object, manner, and degree of distortion. Ideological views of the modern capitalist state can serve to illustrate this point. As seen from the upper strata of the social pyramid, the state mistakenly appears to be the dispassionate defender of general interests and civic equality. From "below" there is of course a better picture of particular interests and privilege, only this perspective is generally somewhat *simplified* in that it is not in a position to detect even the slightest degree of universality and equality.

4. The Trap of "Objective" Meaning and "Objective" Responsibility

The Stalinist "dialectic" of historical action, with its concepts of "objective meaning" and "objective responsibility," is most helpful in revealing some of the typical ways in which ideological distortion comes about.

The Stalinist consciousness is permanently adopted to a metaphysical structure of history which defines *a priori* the meaning of all revolutionary and counterrevolutionary acts. Only within the confines of an historical process so conceived, with its basic components classified in advance, do these acts become meaningful.

The Party, as the revolutionary subject, is the absolute on the basis of which all else can be defined as an antisubject. From this vicious circle of Stalinist-Manichaean polarization it is exceedingly difficult to escape. Any intention of offering resistance to such a party for the sake of revolutionary-humanist goals and personal dignity has come to ruin on the shoals of the Stalinist view of "objective" meaning and responsibility. Capitulate to the party—or by your very resistance aid the enemy once again! This, in Leszek Kolakowski's phrase, is "Stalinist blackmail by alternative"—and it is clear that double negation here is not a possibility.

The origins of this preoccupation with the enemy appeared among Marxist thinkers long before the phenomenon of Stalinism. From Bebel to the present day, many Marxists have lived in terror of doing something from which the enemy might benefit. But the real tragedy came with Stalinism, when the enemy was arrayed to the left and to the right, both close to the party line and far from it as well. The enemy was everywhere, even in communist ranks.

In such an environment a communist cannot *by definition* take a single step beyond the strict party line without serving the enemy. He believes that the most innocent disagreement among communists opens a crack which the enemy can easily exploit and deepen into an unbridgeable chasm. To prevent this, the Stalinist hierarchy devised a precise division of labor. It secured itself a total monopoly on defining the party line and left it to the membership to worry about falling into the class enemy's clutches.

Thus the Stalinized communist must choose: either to execute all directives obediently, or to become an enemy oneself. Of course the party has fellow-travelers and allies. But once one joins the party there is no returning to fellow-traveler or allied status; there are only "enemies" to join.

Stalinist "dialecticians" do not acknowledge the existence of real *internal* contradictions in their society, much less contradictions that might generate a revolutionary movement. All internal contradictions are "unmasked" as *external* by means of retrospective interpretation. The only other place where we come across such an undialectical picture of the perfect absence of internal conflict is in the thought of certain mystics.

Man does not act in a vacuum: strictly speaking he is not capable of making a single move from which he might benefit without also creating an undesired effect. Abusing this ambiguity, which is characteristic of the human situation, the Stalinist leadership is able to press even contradictory accusations. Thus one aids the enemy by exhibiting excessive zeal in implementing the leadership's decision just as well as when one sabotages its policies. Here a peculiar "dialectic" is at work: the "left deviation" meets the "right deviation." But as Aldous Huxley might say, "extremes meet. For the good reason that they were made to meet."[7]

And in the final analysis all enemies are of the same cloth. Like the party, they too possess a metaphysical-substantial and an empirical-accidental dimension. Differences and conflicts among enemies are allegedly encountered only at a superficial level. The "identity of enemies of all stripes" flows, of course, from the supposed essential consistency and oneness of the party, even when its policy undergoes decisive shifts and reversals.

It should be kept in mind that for the Stalinists every statement is a practical act. For them the "objective meaning" of a statement can be defined by its entire *situational* context, even to the extent that this context assumes greater importance than the statement's content. This reveals unlimited possibilities for arbitrary definitions of a statement's "objective" meaning and consequently for assessing responsibility for it. Everything else becomes more valuable than the statement itself—its author's life history, the reaction and life story of the listener or reader, the circumstances in which the statement was made, its "background," eventual uses and abuses, etc.

Among Stalinists the question of real meaning and truthfulness faded before their concern over who would benefit by a given statement. "Every word we utter, a Communist told me, is not simply a word but an action as well. Therefore we should first ask ourselves not whether it is exact but whom it will profit. Marxists have always been concerned with the objective meaning of their discourse, but earlier they were able to believe that the course of events was on their side, which afforded them a degree of freedom. Truth was also a force."[8]

When a communist embraces the Stalinist concepts of objective meaning and responsibility out of a desire to transcend his subjectivity, he falls straight into the net of party subjectivism and voluntarism. Consequences, of course, do not in themselves make the significance of a human act objective. Someone must affirm them and endow them with specific sense and meaning. For that meaning to be truly objective, it must be the result of careful inquiry and not of an *a priori* deduction. The consequences ought to be sought out or anticipated, compared and ranked, as precisely as possible. Only then can one calculate the balance of objective meaning.

Representatives of the Stalinist party proceed precisely the other way around. Instead of discovering objective meaning, they construct it willfully by means of the *arbitrary* separation, combination, and ranking of consequences. This entirely secondary, incidental, and even merely potential consequences come to the fore under the wing of "objective meaning" and "objective responsibility." The very concept of a consequence is itself often abused, while pure coincidence, circumstance, and accident are described as consequences of the fallen communist's activity.

All this results in the total alienation of the meaning of a given human act and of responsibility for it. There is no better example of objectification which is transformed into alienation. The Stalinized communist withdraws from equal participation in the proces of defining the objective meaning of his own acts and objective responsibility for them, unreservedly transferring that right to the party hierarchy. The inevitable result is that on the ruins of the individual subject there is erected a "collective" subject with its own pseudo-objectivity. This hierarchicalized objectivity, of course, is identical with hierarchicalized subjectivity. Historically this led to a situation in which only one person, the occupant of the summit, was a subject. There can be no effective protection against the alienation of the party, including the alienation of meaning and responsibility, so long as the party is hypostatized and conceived as an entity which is more than the sum of its members, their interpersonal relationships and their activity.

The frequent Stalinist campaigns against "objectivism" in philosophy and science were only superficially at variance with this constant insistence on objective meaning and objective responsibility. Careful analysis, however, will show that these campaigns were directed against the strivings of theorists and investigators for true objectivity and were thus an explicit manifestation of Stalinist party-mindedness. True objectivity presupposes adequacy to that which is being investigated, as well as a true intersubjectivity that excludes the abdication of one subject to the benefit of another.

The retreat of the individual subject before the subjectivism of the party hierarchy is also promoted by the Stalinized communist's obliviousness to the conduct of the leadership which, when evaluating its own policies, acts contrary to the principle of objective meaning and objective responsibility. In this case it lays the stress on *intended* consequences, i.e. on subjective meaning and subjective responsibility.

The Stalinized communist does not call into question the objective meaning of the concepts of objective meaning and objective responsibility being analyzed here, nor does he ask about the objective responsibility of those who advance them. But there is no doubt that the mystification of these notions contributed to the Stalinist degeneration of the communist movement and thereby objectively benefited the opponents of socialism.

* * *

The indecisiveness of Stalin's opponents in the Bolshevik Party during the 1920s is explained in part by their fear that in rejecting Stalin and his followers they would *objectively* be playing into the hands of their enemies. For the same reason some of Stalin's collaborators, once they began to come to their senses, preferred to choose suicide or reconciled themselves to their fate. It was a rare individual who confronted the real question before it was too late: will not the enemy benefit more if Stalin wins? And indeed it was soon to be shown that all these enemies together could not accomplish more than Stalin did in compromising socialism and Marxism.

Mystification in the form of "objective" meaning played a much more direct role in the defeat of the opposition. It is commonly maintained that the opposition tied its hands in advance when at the Tenth Congress it agreed to the ban on factions—an action which was, to be sure, seen as temporary in character. Stalin exploited the ban skillfully. But even *under these conditions* various oppositional currents could have united against him, but did not. Why?

Somewhat more light is shed on this question by the following event:

On 11 July 1928 Bukharin had a secret meeting with Kamenev, organized by Sokolnikov. Kamenev made a résumé of the conversation, which finally leaked and was published abroad. Bukharin had finally seen, as he said, that the political divergences between his own Right-wing faction and the Left-wing faction of Zinoviev and Kamenev were as nothing compared with the *total divergence of principle which separated them all from Stalin.* It was not a question of ideas, since Stalin did not have any. *'He changes his theories according to the need he has of getting rid of somebody at such-and-such a moment.'*

Confronted with their own powerlessness the oppositionists, we find, finally posed the question: *what kind of a person was Stalin?* Previously they had exhausted themselves in mutual recriminations and alternating support of Stalin's tactical zig-zags. Bukharin's right wing had supported him in his struggle against the Left because it had proceeded from the "objective meaning" of his current policies. But when Stalin later turned against the Right Opposition, the Left paid the Right back in kind not so much out of vengeance as out of a belief that he had finally "objectively" adopted their platform. Thus did the opposition enable Stalin to outmanipulate and outplay it.

Only then did the opposition have serious second thoughts about Stalin's *intentions.* But only on the basis of intentions (and motives), not on the basis of the consequences independently of them, can we penetrate to the disposition of the actor under examination here. In his "Testament" Lenin warned of the role that could be played by Stalin's character defects. To be sure, not even he suspected how *immeasurable* a potential for evil already existed in Stalin's personality.

The young Lukács were keenly aware of the danger that threatened Marxism from the beginning of underestimating the importance of actors' intentions and motives:

However, we have now reached the point at which the dangerous sides of Hegel's legacy appear in Marxism. In Hegel's system there is no ethics. In Hegel ethics is replaced by a system of material, spiritual, and social goods in which his philosophy of society culminates. Marxism has in essence adopted this form of ethics (for example, Kautsky's book), only in place of Hegel's it has put other "values," neglecting the question of whether the striving for socially correct "values" and socially correct goals — independently of the *internal* springs of action — is in itself ethical, even though it is obvious that an ethical question can only be posed from the standpoint of those socially correct goals. He who refuses to analyze the ethical question given here also denies its ethical possibility and thus falls prey to contradiction by the most primitive and universal social facts: conscience and consciousness of responsibility. These are not concerned with first asking *what* a person did or wanted (this, namely, is affirmed by the norms of social and political action), but rather with *why* he did what he did or wanted what he wanted, whether or not his action or desire was objectively correct. This question, *why,* can appear only in the case of the individual, for it is meaningful only in relation to the individual and stands in sharp contrast to the tactical question of objective correctness, which can be resolved only in the collective action of human groups. Thus the question before us is as follows: how are consciousness and the sense of individual responsibility related to the problems of tactically correct collective action?[10]

While the concept of action has become further enriched under the wing of other theories, in official Marxism it has become all the more impoverished. The conceptual repertoire of Marxism relating to action has gradually been all but reduced to the notion of subjective and objective meaning (and responsibility). Moreover, out of a fear of moralistic subjectivism the emphasis has been laid on the "objective" side of this formula. It is assumed that the evaluation of intentions in politics is not so important, for the road to hell is paved with good intentions. But in doing so one loses sight of the fact that the road to hell is *covered* with evil intentions. In politics one must guard against a twofold naiveté. A theory of action and ethics which underestimates the importance of intentions and motives is just as immature in political matters as one which commits the same error with regard to consequences.

5. Maurice Merleau-Ponty's Concepts of "Historical Meaning" and "Historical Responsibility"

The Marxist who wishes to develop a theory and ethics of revolutionary action must critically examine Merleau-Ponty's collection of essays, *Humanism and Terror,* originally published in 1947. Returning ten years into the past to the Moscow trials of the Bolshevik leaders, he decisively rejects the verdicts according to which the defendants' "subjective treason" was proved in ostensibly normal court proceedings. Nor can there be any talk of "true justice" in this instance. This does not mean, however, says Merleau-Ponty, that the attacks on the trials by Trotsky, Koestler, and the liberal humanists—who argued for the "subjective innocence" of the accused and accordingly pointed to the "legal crimes" committed against them—were on the mark.

Solely by proceeding from *historical meaning and responsibility* as well as *revolutionary justice* is it possible, according to Merleau-Ponty, to penetrate to the truth of these verdicts. Let us permit him to speak for himself.

On one occasion Stalin made the following pronouncement: "All the Trotskyite and rightist machinations against its Party and their entire wrecking 'activity' directed against our government's policies has only one aim: to destroy the Party's program and delay the task of industrialization and collectivization." Merleau-Ponty cites this and comments: "*Instead* of saying 'had only one aim,' let us say 'could only have one result,' or 'one meaning,' and the discussion is closed."[11]

If at the time of the Moscow trials *there was still no specific* historical meaning and, similarly, historical responsibility of the accused for their opposition to the Stalinist industrialization and collectivization and the imposition of absolute discipline in the party and in the country as a whole, then with the Nazi attack on the USSR and her role in the Second World War it *became certain in retrospect,* according to Merleau-Ponty, that the oppositionists' politics *objectively signified treason.* This is *history's judgment.* "Whatever the opposition may have wanted and even if it was a more certain future for the Revolution, it remains that *in fact it weakened the U.S.S.R.* In any case, *by one of those sudden reversals so frequent in history, the events of 1941 accuse them of treason.*"[12]

It is easy to give in to the temptation of concluding too hastily that it is inappropriate to discuss the Moscow trials and Merleau-Ponty's interpretation of them when it has been even officially acknowledged by the Soviet leadership that they were staged. Yet Merleau-Ponty did not, for that matter, assert that the confessions of the accused were credible.

A merely factual examination alone of Merleau-Ponty's interpretation would indeed be meaningless in light of what we now know about the trials. We must concentrate, therefore, on his *theoretical categories and the manner in which he applies them.* In this context "historical responsibility" is of critical importance:

> Historical responsibility transcends the categories of liberal thought—intention and act, circumstances and will, objective and subjective. It overwhelms the individual in his acts, mingles the objective and subjective, *imputes circumstances to his will; thus it substitutes for the individual as he feels himself to be a role or phantom in which he cannot recognize himself, but in which he must see himself. . . .*[13]

> To govern, it has to be said, is to foresee, and the politician cannot excuse himself for what he has not foreseen. Yet, there is always the *unforeseeable.* There is the tragedy.[14]

> *It is the nightmare of an involuntary responsibility and guilt by circumstance which already underlies the Oedipus myth. . . .* The whole of Greek tragedy assumes this idea of an *essential contingency through which we are all guilty and all innocent because we do not know what we are doing.*[15]

> The purges resume and concentrate the paradox of history which is that a *contingent future,* once it enters the present, appears real and even necessary. There appears here a *harsh notion of responsibility, based not on what men intended but what they find they have achieved in the light of the event.*[16]

But the problem is not merely that Merleau-Ponty imposes a "harsh" notion of responsibility; it is in fact insupportable. A brief digression will bring us to an explanation of this assessment.

* * *

To the less attentive reader it might seem that Merleau-Ponty's concept of historical responsibility is identical to the Stalinist idea of objective responsibility. Objective meaning and responsibility are defined for Stalinists by the *a priori* and inexorable structure of the course of history. The party is the absolute expert and judge which, from a history full of meaning, recasts that meaning into human acts and measures responsibility accordingly. Stalinists believe that Marxism puts at their disposal an infallible science not only of what has already occurred, but of the future as well. As Camus put it in *The Rebel,* they "alone are capable of reading in history the meaning with which they previously endowed it."[17] "In the new universe, on the other hand, the judgment pronounced by history must be pronounced immediately."[18]

At the core of Merleau-Ponty's vision of the social process is the principle of the *ambiguity of history.* History is neither determined nor scientifically predictable; rather, it is totally uncertain. It constantly changes its face, even having more than one face at any given moment. History's judgment regarding the meaning of an act, and responsibility for it, is relative since it depends to a considerable degree on historical contingencies. Under the influence of Merleau-Ponty, among others, the idea of the ambiguity of history achieved considerable popularity in the 1940s and 1950s, in part at the expense of the unilinear and rigid determinism so characteristic of Stalinist Marxism.

While the Stalinist conception of the meaning of the human act has arrogant pretensions to absolutism because it *de facto* conceals relativism, Merleau-Ponty prides himself on the relativism of his approach to history. At the time of the purges in the USSR it was often said among the Stalinists that the earlier "sins" of the opposition must be "translated into the language of 1937." Merleau-Ponty makes this translation, but in the language of 1941. Beyond this, in line with his idea of the ambiguity of history, he allows: "Like the Church, the Party will perhaps rehabilitate those whom it condemned once a new historical phase has altered the significance of their behavior."[19] Fanatical Stalinists would never admit of such a possibility, however much they might (ab)use the principle of historical relativity, as when the reactionary conquests of the Russian Tsars were presented in historical perspective as progressive since they had indirectly contributed to the greatness of the Soviet land.

What is the status of the response to the question of determinism in history with respect to our understanding of the historical actor's responsibility? On this count, too, it is worth comparing the Stalinists with Merleau-Ponty.

Stalinist ideologists are strong proponents of historical determinism. And for this very reason we would expect them to reduce human responsibility to a minimum. But as logical coherence was never the strongest point of Stalinist ideology, *the more determinism, the more responsibility.* The Stalinist's ideological reliance on historical inevitability is most often accompanied in practice by a voluntaristic meting out of responsibility. Whenever required by political circumstance, the Stalinists can make an individual more responsible than can the proponents of any other ideology. In order to bridge the chasm between hyper–determinism and hyper–responsibility they rely on the notion of "objective" meaning, faith in the unlimited power of Marxist prediction of the outcome of historical action, and the definition of freedom as "recognized necessity." And this last element bears witness to the way in which a philosophical idea (Spinoza, Hegel, Engels) can successfully be reworked and exploited for an ideological purpose.

Marx, in writing the following lines, almost seems to have been warning in advance against such abuses of his thought:

> *My standpoint,* from which the evolution of the economic formation of society is viewed as a process of natural history, *can less than any other make the individual responsible for relations whose creature he socially remains,* however much he may subjectively raise himself above them.[20]

Indeed, and most logically—*the more determinism and necessity, the less responsibility.*

As we have seen, Merleau-Ponty decisively rejects the idea of the determined nature of the course of history. On the basis of this negative orientation it might seem that he would have no difficulty in insisting on freedom of responsibility. What, however, is his positive definition of the openness and uncertainty of history? Man unavoidably achieves not only unintended but also unforeseeable results which, together with other results, constitute the historical significance of his actions. We also know that Merleau-Ponty holds man responsible for that entire significance. It turns out that *historical actors are also responsible for consequences which are unforeseeable and beyond their control.*

In vain does Merleau-Ponty strive to convince us that all this is consistent with "strict Marxist method."[21] His solution ultimately has the same effect as the Stalinist one. In both cases, one answers for that which is not dependent on man. In this light it is less important that Merleau-Ponty sees man as confronted primarily by the accidents and reversals of history, while the Stalinists see him as confronted by social regularities (which are most often the mystification of party reversals).

* * *

In a later work Merleau-Ponty states:

> The philosopher recognizes himself by the fact that he *simultaneously* has a sense for evidence as well as a feeling for ambiguity. When he limits himself to

tolerating ambiguity, it is called equivocation. In the great philosophers ambiguity becomes a theme and contributes to the establishment of certainty, instead of jeopardizing that certainty. Therefore *a distinction must be made between good and bad ambiguity.*[22]

Let me put it this way: the concept of the ambiguity of history as applied in Merleau-Ponty's book represents *bad ambiguity.* Alluding to the title of one of his later books, it also would not be an exaggeration to say that Merleau-Ponty himself was a victim of the "adventures of the dialectic."

He persuasively depicts a drama that results from "the general structure of human action," particularly historical action. The "tragic consciousness" knows and is tormented in its knowledge that its undertakings *inevitably* acquire a divergent and even contrary meaning to what was intended, foreseen, and foreseeable. The totally innocent actor is crucified between intended, foreseen, and foreseeable outcomes (one meaning) and results contrary to them (a second meaning). Thus *the human act can simultaneously have and lack a given meaning.* This is an example of "good ambiguity."

Needless to say, we can only try to reduce this alienation of action but we can never totally eliminate it. But if this is the case on the individual level, how much more so on that of humanity and history! Sartre is right when he says: "Thus man makes History; this means that he objectifies himself in it and is alienated in it. In this sense History, which is the proper work of *all* activity and of *all* men, appears to men as a foreign force exactly insofar as they do not recognize the meaning of their enterprise. . . ."[23] But from this Sartre immediately leaps uncontrollably to the superutopia of the existence of "only one meaning" of history in the future:

> Thus the plurality of *the meanings* of History can be discovered and posited for itself only upon the ground of a future totalization—in terms of the future totalization and in contradiction with it. It is our theoretical and practical duty to bring this totalization closer every day. . . . Our historical task, at the heart of this polyvalent world, is to bring closer the moment when History will have *only one meaning*, when it will tend to be dissolved in the concrete men who will make it in common.[24]

But let us return to Merleau-Ponty. In extrapolating the ambiguity of the meaning of a given act he also formulates the ambiguity of responsibility for that act. *The individual can be simultaneously innocent and guilty:* the former by intention, the latter in terms of result. But there are results and results: intended and unintended, foreseen and unforeseen, foreseeable and unforeseeable. Insofar as he did not sufficiently honor these distinctions in defining his notion of responsibility, Merleau-Ponty has proposed a "bad ambiguity." The individual can indeed be innocent (subjectively) in the sense that he intended and foresaw certain consequences, and at the same instant guilty (objectively) insofar as he brought about other, undesirable consequences, but only if these were foreseeable. This is how a "bad ambiguity" gets transformed into an untruthful assertion about responsibility for unforeseeable consequences as well.

The "historical meaning" (sense) of an act depends upon its consequences: intended and unintended, short-term and long-term, direct and indirect, foreseeable and unforeseeable, etc. Since the totality of consequences is never definitively circumscribed, "historical meaning" is subject to constant change. Thus arises its paradox. Where does *real* "historical meaning," or at least that meaning which is *more real* than others, begin and end? We are truly threatened by the danger that human actions are so burdened down with "historical meaning" that they become quite senseless. The very notion of meaning or sense suggests that we are speaking of something that is at least relatively defined and finite.

From the foregoing it need not be concluded that the category of "historical meaning" is useless. But the weaknesses and dangers which lurk under the wings of that notion should constantly be taken into account. The worst of these dangers is the use of this concept in promoting the mystification of the noble sense of "historical responsibility." But this is precisely what Merleau-Ponty does when he confronts the revolutionary with a narrow choice: either responsibility only for intended consequences, which would obviously be insupportable subjectivism, or responsibility for all consequences, which is allegedly an inseparable component of all activism and most of all revolutionary activism. The author's logic is evidently insurmountable: as fighters who try to be much more than "beautiful souls," revolutionaries must assume responsibility for the *entire* meaning of their actions, objectively as well as subjectively.

Had he defined "historical responsibility" independently of "historical meaning," Merleau-Ponty would most likely not have made this mistake. From the fact that the "historical meaning" of an act can comprise *all* its consequences (up to a specific moment, of course) it does not at all follow that the same holds for the "historical responsibility" of the actor. It has long been the case that neither reason nor sentiment have dictated that anyone assume responsibility for *unforeseeable* consequences. "Historical meaning" is too broad for us to be able to identify it with the responsibility of any mortal being, even a revolutionary. Otherwise the responsibility of the actor would change continuously with the boundlessly fluid "historical meaning" of the act. In order to encompass unforeseeable consequences under the rubric of "historical responsibility," Merleau-Ponty first refracts them through the prism of "historical meaning."

But while the potential for divergence among intentions, predictions, and results is truly *inherent in the structure of human action,* the concept of responsibility is a matter of socio-historical *development and choice.* By being assigned responsibility for the total result of his action, man is degraded to being a link in the chain of cause and effect. In this case, participation in the production of effects is transformed from a *necessary* to a *sufficient* condition of responsibility. Is man not reified in this line of reasoning?

Merleau-Ponty confronts the subjectivism of Stalinism with intersubjectivity. No one is privileged in the eyes of history: historical meaning and historical responsibility, both for Stalinist and anti-Stalinist policies alike, depend equally on the fickle moods of the historical process. Through critical analysis we have found that the abdication of the individual subject before the party hierarchy is characteristic of Stalinism. Therefore Merleau-Ponty is right when he reproaches Stalinism for the total absence of intersubjectivity. But he anticipates that true intersubjectivity presupposes not only that the subjects of action be equal, but also that no subject be treated merely as a physical being or cause. But by broadening responsibility to include unforeseeable consequences, Merleau-Ponty commits precisely this latter error.

In discussions of the relationship between morality and politics it is customary to stress that the *ethics of intention* (and motive) is inappropriate for the evaluation of political activity. Does this mean that in the sphere of politics we must embrace the opposite extreme — *the ethics of efficiency?*

In analyzing the conflict between Stalin and the opposition we have already seen how serious the consequences of neglecting the intentions and motives of political actors can be. Thus political ethics requires that we try to synthesize both components.

Is it, however, perhaps the case that *political* responsibility differs from *moral* responsibility in that it comprises the unforeseeable aspect of action as well? Such overtones are audible in Merleau-Ponty, particularly when he speaks of the responsibility of political leaders.

Political activity indeed has a colossal impact on the lives of an enormous number of people. The politician's responsibility is great because his power is exceptionally great. He is responsible for those consequences which he failed to foresee through haste or heedless aggressiveness as well as others. The politician cannot escape responsibility when his actions lead to situations that he cannot control, even though he is not responsible for every individual evil that arises in these situations. "The early Christians knew full well the world is governed by demons and that he who lets himself in for politics, that is, for power and force as means, contracts with diabolical powers and for his action it is *not* true that good can follow only from good and evil only from evil, but that often the opposite is true."[25]

It hardly needs to be emphasized that all this is not an acceptable justification for politicians who are agents of the status quo. They, indeed, take no risks of venturing into the unknown, but they are responsible for defending or at least tolerating existing evil.

Nor does anyone dispute the fact that the criterion of successfulness is regularly applied to political activity. In politics there truly exists a need to evaluate *all* consequences. In this spirit Merleau-Ponty writes: "We have never said that any policy which succeeds is good. We said that *in order to be good a policy must succeed.*"[26]

Yet Merleau-Ponty nowhere separates the *evaluation of the political act* (good-bad, successful-unsuccessful) *on the basis of its total outcome* from the *evaluation of the actor's responsibility for that outcome. The latter sort of evaluation is limited only to the foreseeable part of the outcome.* Here is an illustration of the former type of assessment:

> A leader's achievement must at some point be judged in terms of success or failure, but such judgments will vary with the time perspective. Stanley Hoffman once observed that "Metternich had succeeded by 1825 and failed by 1848; and writers disagree whether he had succeeded or failed by 1914."[27]

In the interpersonal clashes of political opponents, to be sure, a distinction is not usually made between the two types of evaluations described above; each opponent points to the totality of consequences of the policies he is attacking. But not even in this case will he *admit* that he is blaming his opponent for unforeseeable consequences.

In no way do I wish to create the impression that I think it is easy to define criteria for the predictability of the consequences of human activity. We are still far from a satisfactory solution to this question, although the books devoted to it would fill whole libraries. There are three possibilities. First, we can take into consideration only that which the actor, *such as he is,* could foresee. But in this case we would fail to require that the actor be fully conscientious in his actions. Thus the second solution would comprise all that which the actor could have foreseen *had he exerted himself to learn as much as possible.* However, where are we to draw the line between what he was obliged to learn and what he was not? The third solution would avoid this difficulty by insisting on all that was foreseeable proceeding from the *achieved level of human knowledge.* But from how many people could anything of this nature be realistically expected? As ought to be apparent, in any event, to delve into all these questions a separate book would be necessary.

* * *

To this point we have been analyzing Merleau-Ponty's categories in the abstract. Now we need to inquire as to the result when they are applied to the interpretation of the Moscow trials. Let us begin by citing some statements which are, to put it mildly, surprising:

> Guilt in this case *is not a matter of a clear relation* between a definite act with specific motives and specific consequences.[28]

The chain of causes, motives, means, and effects of the opposition's activity *is not reconstructed.* There are *only a few facts in a fog of shifting meanings.*[29]

Thus *the smallest detail acquires an immense significance.*[30]

Is it really possible, after these assertions, to speak at all of any sort of historical meaning and historical responsibility? I will say without hesitation that they should above all be called *pseudo-historical,* just as I have characterized objective meaning and objective responsibility in the Stalinist variant as *pseudo-objective.* For the same reasons it is clear that the Moscow trials were not, as Merleau-Ponty asserts, an expression of revolutionary justice, but rather a tragic parody of justice in any sense of the term.

With respect to his ideas concerning historical meaning and historical responsibility, we might have expected Merleau-Ponty to insist on the crucial question of factual evidence: what did the opposition *really* do and what were the *real* consequences of its activity? But he does not do this and even fundamentally alters his own definition of historical meaning and historical responsibility without even noting that he is doing so:

As long as there are men, a society, and an open history, such conflicts remain a possibility and our historical or objective responsibility is *only our responsibility in the eyes of other men.*[31]

When Bukharin was tried the enemy was no longer or not yet on Soviet soil. But in a country which since 1917 had known only extreme situations, even before the war and the invasion, *opposition could well look like treason.*[32]

Thus it turns out that the opposition's historical responsibility is measured not by what it really did and the real consequences of its activity, but by *how it was viewed* by its Stalinist accusers! How else to explain the fact that the author holds that what was on trial was "an organized opposition which aims at the overthrow of the revolutionary leadership,"[33] although it was an historical fact that in the prisoners' dock were adherents of a former opposition who had publicly recanted and, thus broken, nearly to a man had placed themselves in Stalin's service.

Without this ambiguity in his concept of responsibility it is also impossible to understand why the author, in his Introduction, defends himself from criticism by asserting, "We have not examined whether in fact Bukharin led an organized opposition. . . ."[34]

Does Merleau-Ponty act in accordance with his own methodological-dialectical principle? "[T]he crime has to be set in the logic of a situation, in the dynamics of a regime and into the *historical totality* to which it belongs, instead of judging it by itself according to that morality mistakenly called 'pure' morality."[35] This point of departure obliged Merleau-Ponty to be careful to affirm the character and consequences of the Stalinist regime's activity as well as that of the former opposition, to compare them and only then to define the historical meaning and responsibility of both parties.

Merleau-Ponty has done none of this. Had he done so, he would have noted that Stalinism itself in no small way brought about the USSR's collapse in 1941, for the following reasons: mass terror in a country in which the best party, army, administrative, economic, and intellectual cadres were wiped out; the transformation of communist parties the world over into followers of changing Soviet policies, as a result of which Nazism's rise to power was facilitated and any effective communist resistance to Nazi aggression was made impossible in nearly every country; Great-Russian hegemonism which evoked enormous disaffection among the other nations of the USSR; and thick-skulled Stalinist illusions concerning Hitler's immediate intentions toward the USSR. Many more such catastrophic effects of Stalinism could be cited as well.

It is odd that Merleau-Ponty took none of this seriously into account, although he otherwise entertained no great illusions about Stalinism as a system. He himself has defined it in the following manner: increased social hierarchy; an unimportant social role played by the proletariat; political disagreements depicted as crimes and punished by death; increased wage differentials; no sign of the withering away of the state, and instead an ever enlarging dictatorial apparatus; and methodical lying, mistrust, and corruption increasingly becoming systemic characteristics.

It is natural that Merleau-Ponty was extremely upset by charges that his work constituted an apologia for the legal crimes of Stalinism. He vigorously protested these accusations in the Introduction to the set of essays from which we shall presently be taking our leave.

It is entirely accurate that he never asserted that "it was necessary to condemn Bukharin nor that the Trials were justified by Stalingrad,"[36] much less that "the execution of the Old Bolsheviks was really indispensable to the order and national defense of the U.S.S.R."[37] These are indeed neither implications nor even explications of Merleau-Ponty.

Merleau-Ponty himself was quite guilty, however, of creating the impression that he had defended Stalinism, since he turned the real problem on its head. In his devotion, that is to say, he threw himself into demonstrating the opposition's historical responsibility for its resistance to Stalinism instead of concentrating on examining the Stalinists' historical responsibility, in doing which he need not have blamed them for a single unforeseeable consequence, as my statement of charges of a moment ago also avoided doing. The oppositionists were truly guilty, not of anti-Stalinism, but of contributing to the creation and maintenance of an authoritarian atmosphere in the Bolshevik Party which most benefited Stalin and his followers; of being unprepared for timely, decisive, and united countermeasures against Stalinism's advance; of the disgraceful capitulation of many of them before Stalin and even of participation in his glorification. . . .

One might have hoped that a philosopher of Merleau-Ponty's talent would have thoroughly illuminated the Stalinist perspective on the opposition. But such hopes would have been in vain, for with his assessment of historical meaning and historical responsibility Merleau-Ponty himself obscured the essence of the Moscow trials. To be sure, he partly demystified them by rejecting the charge of "subjective treason" on the part of the opposition. But Merleau-Ponty's example also shows that partial demystification can contribute to the preservation of mystification. Merleau-Ponty's halfway approach explains why some attack him as a defender of Stalinism while others praise him for anti-Stalinism. Why did he fail to give serious and timely thought to the historical meaning of his theses?

Yet we must not lose sight of the fact that Merleau-Ponty's book is superior to and far more interesting than anything of the Stalinist stamp. It is also refreshing in comparison with Stalinism's shallow moralism in its treatment of political action. The problems he addresses are not simple situations and one-on-one interpersonal relationships, but extremely complicated collective undertakings. The theory and ethics of revolutionary action must truly take into account some of his observations about this type of activity.

6. Between a Metaphysical and Positivistic Attitude Toward the Party

Even when he finds himself confronted with the multitude of proofs of errors, injustices, and even crimes in the party the Stalinized communist still obediently remains a party man. His justification is provided by a peculiar metaphysics of the party. However negative events in the party may be, this still is not seen as characteristic of its substance—the party as such. Or to reverse the proposition, everything that is positive in the party is said to derive from its essence. Were he able to express himself in philosophical terms he would say that the party's essence precedes its existence.

The party's *a priori* essence remains eternally unaffected and above everything in its empirical existence. On the empirical level it is impossible for something so terrible to happen that it could not represent mere accident or, at worst, a stage in the "transitional period." There is no better illustration of this than the response of Klement Gottwald, at the time the Chairman of the Communist Party of Czechoslovakia, to questions from some party members regarding whom to believe after the "treason" of Slansky and other high party leaders: believe the Party. Such untroubled essentialism also emerges from the official critics of the "period of the cult of personality" in the USSR, beginning with Khrushchev's speech at the Twentieth Party Congress.

Andrey Platonov succeeded in giving this unforgettable description of this fetishism of the party:

"'Have you ever seen the Communist Party?'

" 'No, Comrade Pyotr, they've never shown it to me! In the village I only saw Comrade Chumov!'

" 'There are as many Comrade Chumovs as you like here, too. But I'm talking about the *pure Party* which has a precise outlook and a precise viewpoint.' "[38]

Many of those who suffered in the Stalinist purges went off to their deaths explaining their fate as a consequence of some misunderstanding, not as the effect of the true nature of their party. The process of historical development toward the classless society is an *a priori* matter for such a communist and his approach to the issue is ultimately independent of the real course of history. At the same time the party's substance is bound to that historical process in an *a priori* manner as well, for which the actual state of affairs within the party is by definition irrelevant. Therefore a "small" or "factual" truth is in no position whatsoever to besmirch the "great" or "epochal" truth.

Without this metaphysical guarantee of the party's correctness the Stalinized communist would lose his sense of historical mission and his rationale for struggling, and perhaps even living. We may apply to his case one of Marx's thoughts which is particularly appropriate: however great is the party's strength, so great is mine. The party's properties are my properties and essential strengths. That which I am and am not, furthermore, is in no way defined by my individuality . . . and does not, moreover, the party transform my powerlessness into its opposite?[39]

For the Stalinized communist, deserting the party means losing one's link with history. Only with the party does he feel that he enjoys a privileged relationship toward the future. "The truth is that they are like this; they know everything beforehand. They are already aware of how things to come will unfold. The future is far in the past, and for them it is only a repetition."[40] The belief in the historical inevitability of communism inspires him to unprecedented activism, but at the same time makes him powerless before the party. Once in the party he burns all bridges behind him. Could he possibly do the same with the bridge that surely leads to utopia?! What is the individual's dignity in comparison with its brilliance? But this is a strange type of utopian consciousness: for him *topos* is ultimately more important than *u-topos*.

It might be anticipated that this consciousness of the *separation* (when it comes to justifying the party) of the metaphysical and empirical dimensions would not only save one from the abyss of despair but also inspire one to rebel against the empirical whenever it is in opposition to the metaphysical. But this consciousness is once again inconsistent: as soon as it falls under the party's sway it immediately makes these two levels *identical,* and this to the benefit of the empirical, as if there were some pre-stability harmony between them. Thus the party's metaphysical side does not save the Stalinist consciousness from an altogether empirical capitulation.

In this way unbounded devotion to the revolutionary cause degenerates into blind obedience to the victors in the heedless struggle for party dominance.

This is the consequence of reductive transformations—the revolutionary cause of the proletariat is identified with the revolutionary movement, and the movement is identified with the party, which in turn is identified with the victorious faction. The existing leadership always embodies the party's essence. The Stalinized communist always obeys it, although he knows very well that it has not come to power by anything resembling democratic means.

The fear of factionalism assumed oppressive proportions in the Stalinized parties. Nor is it at all strange that communists reared on the *Short Course of the History of the CPSU(b)* should have been unable to learn that Lenin fractiously split the party whenever he believed he was right, even though he may have been in the minority. Stalinism arrogated to itself the right of the ruling faction to orchestrate the humiliating recantations of adherents of the defeated faction, and even the stamp of "factionalism" was retroactively reserved exclusively for the vanquished. While appealing to the party's transempirical dimension, the leadership often fundamentally altered its composition by means of the purge. When something in the party is not quite right—change the membership.

While he may appeal to some "logic" (of history), this type of communist understands that the measure applied to him conflicts with that used for the party hierarchy. If he is "objectively" to blame for something, the reason must be sought in his non-proletarian origins or even in the direct influence of the enemy. And should he not confess his guilt, this is immediately interpreted as the result of his own hostile nature, which had hitherto been concealed from the party. The only thing that does not come to mind is that the Stalinized communist would seek the enemy's succor precisely because of the party hierarchy's charges.

7. The Knout of Reaction

The very first undignified act of the Stalinized communist opens up a moral void which quickly expands. The most difficult thing is to cross this boundary. Further deterioration is more a matter of degree than of principle. After this the remaining defenses rapidly fall away. This Moloch is insatiable: obeisances evoke only his contempt and demand for total capitulation.

Once it sets in, the effects of this deterioration accumulate and manifest themselves in the form of habituation to self-abasement. When he no longer has the strength to resist, moreover, this communist will be inclined to throw himself with nearly sadistic force on those who do offer resistance. And how could it be otherwise, when they remind him of his abandoned human potentialities? "The spectacle of human pride is incomparable."[41] How can one suppress the feeling of shame in the presence of those who jealously guard their moral integrity? They must be drawn after oneself into the quicksand of self-abasement at any price. "Whatever goes upon two legs is an enemy."[42]

The extent of the danger represented by those who conduct themselves with dignity before the party is illustrated by the persistence with which the Stalinists try to break a man. Expulsions are insufficient; self-abasement is required as well. Stalinists accurately sense that control over people is total only when their dignity is overcome, since dignity endows the core of the human personality with value. The most important goal of the Moscow trials was exultation over the defendants' self-degradation, not their physical annihilation and the terrorizing of others, for this could have been accomplished without the public spectacles as well. The former oppositionists became totally harmless only once they had irrevocably affirmed in court that they lacked the strength to act in a revolutionary manner.

In a certain sense Stalin appreciated the significance of moral example in the political struggle more accurately than the oppositionists. They miscalculated in believing that by the ruse of "limited self-criticism" they could avoid further attacks and preserve their chances in the struggle against Stalin. Let us return to the self-critical declaration by the opposition's leaders of October 17, 1926, which we cited in Part I of this book. They stated that they had not changed their views but were rejecting factional activity and appealing to their followers to do the same. Trotsky later explained this[43] as a tactical step and a signal to the membership that they wanted to continue the struggle within the Party and not outside of it. But the self-criticizers underestimated the fact that they were participating in a game whose rules were being dictated by the other side. And this meant that their true intentions had to remain unarticulated and they were therefore unable to neutralize the impression created by their humiliating retreat.

Stalin immediately stepped up the pressure:

> But Stalin knew that it was not enough to defeat opponents: one must force them to debase themselves. . . . Previously, such self-abasement had been the price for being allowed to remain in the party; now it had to be paid for a mere hope of readmission. Shortly before the decisive vote was taken, Stalin made the opposition "an explicit offer: if the capitulation was complete enough, expulsions from the party would be limited in time—readmissions would be considered later—and the bloc leaders would be allowed to remain in Moscow." Zinoviev and Kamenev accepted, Trotsky refused. . . .[44]

The first arrests of members of the opposition took place as early as the autumn of 1927. For tactical reasons Stalin would later permit some of its leaders to return to the Party and to leading positions, although to be sure far from the center of power. In the meantime the price was raised with ever greater humiliations being required, along with the public glorification of Stalin. And ultimately not even this saved them from the gallows.

Such behavior, of course, is not new. A great many examples could be cited from the history of Christianity. But this is what befell the leader of a rebellion in China in 1864:

> Li Hsiu-Tseng was executed after a long imprisonment and just as he had finished his memoirs written at the order of Tseng Kuo-Fan, who subsequently corrected them with great care and extraordinary skill — with an acute appreciation of the significance of what would today be called "internal belief" — with the goal of demonstrating how even a leader of a rebellion ended his life acknowledging the moral superiority, invincibility, and great efficiency of the "old order."[45]

In the USSR it all began with "small" self-criticisms and ended a decade later in mass executions. The "ruse" of the self-critical mind fit into the ruse of the dictatorial mind. Public recantations quickly became a universal way of life, and then of death, in Stalinism. I do not doubt that one had to be more visionary than Woland, the professor of black magic in Bulgakov's *The Master and Marguerita,* to foresee even in the 1920s such a horrible end. Reality proved to be incomparably more fantastic and horrible than any writer's negative utopia. We may note in the margins that in the mirror of Stalinist life, not even Dostoyevsky's "demons" acted in such a terrifying manner.

It is worth recalling some instances from the histories of other parties. At the Fourth Congress of the Communist Party of Yugoslavia in Dresden in 1928 Togliatti, the Chairman of the Comintern, demanded "absolute capitulation" of Sima Marković [the leader of the Yugoslav Party at the time: Trans.]. Marković accepted the ultimatum and wrote a self-critical letter to the communists of Belgrade. Later he was killed in the USSR.[46] A postwar example: Slansky first submitted to self-criticism and was removed as General Secretary of the Communist Party of Czechoslovakia and named Deputy Premier of the Government, but in addition he was brought to trial and executed. That men do not, as a rule, learn from history is also seen from the public recantation of Černik, the Premier of the Czechoslovak Government at the time of Dubcek. He, too, was under the illusion that self-criticism would help him after the military intervention, but he was quickly replaced and expelled from the Party — it was a new age and the consequences were significantly milder than at the height of Stalinism.

In classical Stalinism very few of those who had undergone self-criticism survived. György Lukács was one who did, probably because he did not personally arouse Stalin's anger. The retrospective explanation that he offered for his self-critical statements does not seem altogether credible to me since there is not a single word about fear for his own fate. I quote:

> When I heard from a reliable source that Béla Kun was planning to expel me from the Party as a "Liquidator," I gave up the struggle, as I was well aware of Kun's prestige in the International, and I published a "Self-Criticism." I was

indeed firmly convinced that I was in the right but I knew also—e.g. from the fate that had befallen Karl Korsch—that to be expelled from the Party meant that it would no longer be possible to participate actively in the struggle against Fascism. I wrote my self-criticism as an "entry ticket" to such activity as I neither could nor wished to continue to work in the Hungarian movement under the circumstances.[47]

I returned to the Soviet Union in 1933 with every prospect of fruitful activity: the oppositional role of the magazine *Literaturni kritik* on questions of literary theory in the years 1934-1939 is well known. Tactically it was, however, necessary to distance myself publicly from *History and Class Consciousness* so that the real partisan warfare against official and semi-official theories of literature would not be impeded by counter-attacks in which my opponents would have been objectively in the right in my view, however narrow-minded they might otherwise be. Of course, in order to publish a self-criticism it was necessary to adopt the current official jargon. This is the only conformist element in the declaration I made at this time. It too was an entry ticket to all further partisan warfare; the difference between this declaration and my earlier retraction of the Blum Theses is "merely" that I sincerely did believe that *History and Class Consciousness* was mistaken and I think that to this day.[48]

In order to understand the psychology of the powerful and their need to demonstrate their omnipotence in this manner as well, it should not be overlooked that the occasional person who refused to save himself through self-abasement did remain alive. This is how Mikhail Bulgakov acted in his Letter to the Government of March 28, 1930:

After the official ban on all my works, many people who knew me as a writer began suggesting that I write a "Communist play" (the quotation marks are not mine). Furthermore, I was advised to submit a letter of repentance to the Government of the U.S.S.R. renouncing the views expressed in my previous literary works, and giving assurance that henceforth I intended to work as a fellow traveler dedicated to the ideas of Communism. The aim? To save myself from persecution, poverty, and inevitable ruin. . . . I did not heed this advice. It is very doubtful whether I could have appeared in a favorable light in the eyes of the Soviet Government, had I written such a hypocritical letter, which could only have been a superficial one, and indeed a naive political trick. Nor did I try to write a Communist play—since I was sure from the beginning that I would not be able to write such a play with any degree of success.[49]

The whole world now knows that at the height of his power Stalin gave the orders to murder millions of people, among them even Bolsheviks. What was the Night of Saint Bartholomew or the Night of the Long Knives in comparison with these years! The members of the opposition refrained from undertaking sufficiently decisive action because of the "objective meaning" of Stalin's

policies, while he then took his revenge by pressing charges of "subjective treason" (rendering conscious service to the enemy) against them.

Lacking the strength to unmask the Moscow trials, Bukharin nevertheless
insisted on the unbridgeable distance between objective and subjective guilt.
Decisively denying the latter, he tried to preserve at least a minimum of honor.
But it is not fair to say that his conduct elicited greater attention than the
heroism of those Bolsheviks who were unable to be tried in public because they
denied "objective guilt" as well.

Gramsci observed, on one occasion:

> The question arises of whether it is honorable to seek out all the errors in a per-
> son's past in order to confront him with them for the purposes of a current
> polemic. Is it not human to err? Was it not, indeed, through errors that
> today's scientific personages were formed? Is not everyone's biography in
> great part a struggle against the past and an overcoming of the past?[50]

What indeed would Gramsci have said had he known that there were being
prepared Stalinist trials which would not expound on "errors," "indiscretions,"
or "unconscious bourgeois influences," but instead at which "traitors" would
be sentenced? By means of a further elaboration of the procedure that he
described, the root of these "treasons" was sought and found deep in the accused
revolutionary's past. Since the present, according to this conception, can always
throw a fundamentally different light on a revolutionary's life story, the revolutionary is at one blow cast from the history of the revolution to that of the
counterrevolution.

Writers and philosophers are preoccupied with bounded situations. But
there are deaths and there are deaths. What is execution at the hands of the
enemy as compared with the death of a revolutionary, guiltless yet a "traitor,"
at the hands of his erstwhile comrades-in-arms — a superbounded situation?
But here the power of language fails us.

8. Countermeasures

While the Stalinized communist is responsible for the total significance of
his actions — "subjectively" as well as "objectively" — the "party" evaluates his
politics according to his intentions, which is to say subjectively. When it
accuses him of hostile intentions the "party" does this, too, out of revolutionary motives. In his eyes the party has a metaphysical license to prosecute
all failures and deformations, past and future. And he offers no alibi to the
party and must therefore always respond to party criticism by recanting.

At the height of Stalinism this duality was developed to the extreme. Unconditional loyalty was anwered with constant suspicion, and veneration with

contempt. Condescension only reinforced the party hierarchy's arrogance, and adoration stimulated the leadership to demand self-degradation on the part of everyone else.

What is the difference between Stalinist self-criticism and a dignified self-critical posture? In this regard we ask: When the Stalinists themselves insisted so strongly on distinguishing between criticism and "carping criticism," why did they not distinguish between self-criticism and carping self-criticism?

A truly self-critical posture lies in the individual's capacity to be confronted first of all with himself in silent reflection. It requires neither words nor least of all noisy proclamations, for as a *practical* matter it is addressed to future conduct. Just as an individual does not have the moral right to boast of his worth, so he has neither the right nor much less the duty to offer humiliating statements about himself. An intimate sense of self-criticism contributes to the flowering of the personality, while Stalinist self-criticism is a moral gas chamber.

When a proud individual feels the need to compare the results of his self-confrontation with someone else, he will do so in a select circle of his most intimate friends, comrades, and fellow warriors. This would be a type of "dialogical encounter" which for Martin Buber represents an I-Thou, rather than an I-It (object or thing), encounter. No one can plan a truly self-critical "confession," much less officially arrange one, as is otherwise done as a specific agenda item of "criticism and self-criticism" at party meetings. Stalinist self-criticism abuses the longing for revolutionary community. In the Stalinist environment there flourishes only humiliation, hypocrisy, and even masochism.

Stalinist self-criticism is a manifestation of a relationship of subordination and superordination. We can find the greatest degree of insistence on humiliating self-criticism in parties in which the leadership may not be criticized. The possibility that an individual can be subjected to criticism or "talked into" self-criticism is in total conformity with this structure of power.

While the Stalinized communist must accept criticism by the "party" as a peculiar kind of self-criticism, his criticism of the party is never received as party self-criticism but rather, in the best case, as carping criticism and more commonly as a hostile statement. The smaller the party's self-critical capacity, the greater is its insistence on confessional self-criticism on the part of its members. Self-criticism is the sole "privilege" that a member of the Stalinist hierarchy does not utilize so long as he does not have to do so. The Stalinist leadership is constantly praised for its successes, but only rarely does it "acknowledge" its failures, and when it does they are trivial and impersonal. The moment when a powerful figure becomes an object of criticism and begins to engage in self-criticism, we can be sure that he has already been sentenced to fall from power.

The self-criticism of others is an effective instrument in the hands of the hierarchy for "closing the party's ranks." But in those ranks there is room only for those who conform. When the supreme leader takes the exceptional step of making a self-critical statement, he "acknowledges" only that he should have struck much earlier against a given "deviation."

Stalinist self-criticism is most frequently preceded by the pressure of external criticism. If he anticipates such criticism, the party man attempts to dull its thrust in advance through self-criticism. I can conceive of a definition that would be appropriate to this kind of circumstance: dignity is the recognized necessity of self-criticism. Similar acrobatics on the "dialectical" trapeze cost the head of many a Bolshevik.

With time this repressiveness can be internalized to a significant degree. Therefore the concept of *coerced self-criticism* is not a mere contradiction in terms. As a result of the many forms of self-abasement in Stalinism one nearly comes to believe in the existence of a certain *moral thanatos*. Zamyatin would have said, "I have, with regard to the Unified State, the right to accept punishment, and I will not surrender that right to anyone."[51]

The Stalinized communist develops a virtual obsession for self-interrogation and self-purification before the party as if it were his own shadow. "It is so pleasant to sense someone's sharp eye which carefully guards against the slightest mistake, the slightest imprecise step. This may well sound a bit sentimental, but again the same analogy comes to mind: the guardian angels imagined by the ancients. How much of what they dreamed about is materialized in our lives?"[52]

The former Stalinist Richard Wright described a party meeting of the 1930s in Chicago as follows:

> I knew, as I sat there, that there were many people who thought they knew life who had been skeptical of the Moscow trials. But they could not have been skeptical had they witnessed this astonishing trial. Ross had not been doped; he had been awakened. It was not a fear of the Communist Party that had made him confess, but *a fear of the punishment that he would exact of himself* that made him tell of his wrongdoings. The Communists had talked to him until they had given him new eyes with which to see his own crime. And then they sat back and listened to him tell how he had erred. He was one with all the members there, regardless of race or color; his heart was theirs and their hearts were his; and when a man reaches that state of kinship with others, that degree of oneness, or when a trial has made him kin after he has been sundered from them by wrongdoing then he must rise and say, out of a sense of the deepest morality in the world: "I'm guilty. Forgive me."[53]

Confessional self-criticism, moreover, also appears attractive to the Stalinized intellectual because it reminds him of the *self-identification of the offender with the punishment* which Marx, proceeding from Hegel, foresaw for the new society:

> But in *human* relations punishment will *really* be nothing else than the judgment of the offender about himself. People will not want to convince him that

external coercion which others have committed against him is coercion which he has committed against himself. In *other* people he will first of all find natural redeemers from the punishment which he has himself pronounced, i.e. the relationship will be precisely reversed.[54]

Marx defined the relationship of proletarian revolutions to self-criticism in the following manner:

> Bourgeois revolutions, like those of the eighteenth century, storm more swiftly from success to success; their dramatic effects outdo each other; men and things seem set in sparkling brilliants; ecstasy is the everyday spirit: but they are short lived; soon they have attained their zenith, and a long depression lays hold of society before it learns soberly to assimilate the results of its storm and stress period. Proletarian revolutions, on the other hand, like those of the nineteenth century, *criticize themselves constantly,* interrupt themselves continually in their own course, come back to the apparently accomplished in order to begin it afresh, deride with unmerciful thoroughness the inadequacies, weaknesses and paltrinesses of their first attempts, seem to throw down their adversary only in order that he may draw new strength from the earth and rise again more gigantic before them, recoil ever and anon from the indefinite prodigiousness of their own aims, until the situation has been created which makes all turning back impossible, and the conditions themselves cry out:
> Hic Rhodus, hic salta![55]

It is clear that Marx's expectations in this regard are a far cry from (self-) criticism as understood in the Stalinist sense. The latter permits the individual to criticize himself and himself alone, but never the revolution, the party, and its leadership. Such "criticism" and self-criticism was decreed by Zhdanov in 1947 to be a new law of socialist development.

Not even the Stalinized communist is in a position to fall on his knees before other *people* without a total loss of self-respect, but *before the party* the situation is different. Only once he has decoded and demystified the demand that he capitulate "before the party" can he pose the liberating question: what right do *people,* however much they might believe themselves to be of an "exceptional mold," have to seek him to trample upon his own dignity?

Marx's important thought that the "individual man represents the ideal totality of society" might be of great help to the Stalinized communist in this instance. And indeed, if *the individual communist (each one, not only the leaders!) represents the ideal totality of the party,* then the party cannot stand above the communist and cannot require him to bow his head before it. He might also enlist another one of Marx's thoughts in his aid: party life will cast its mystical misty veil from itself only once it is placed under the conscious planned control of freely associated communists as their product. The party as a whole remains opaque to view so long as its adherents also do not understand, to paraphrase Marx, that the Communist Party does nothing. . . . To the contrary, it is the real *communist,* the living communist who does all this . . . . It is not "the communist party" which uses men as a means of achieving — as if it were an individual person — its own ends; it is nothing but the activity of communists in pursuit of their ends.

Otherwise we will find ourselves dealing with a consciousness similar to that which moved a Savonarola. Let us hear his words: "Let God alone act: He is the master who created all the prophets and all the holy men. The master is he who makes a hammer, and after he uses it to do what he needed done, does not return it to the drawer but rather discards it. So He did with Jeremiah; after He used him as much as He wanted, He discarded him and left him to be stoned."[56]

9. On Marxism and Ethics

The reader will not have failed to observe that my critique of Stalinism has an ethical dimension. But, many a Marxist will retort, ethics in general is not possible in Marxism. Therefore I will first try to explicate their arguments and only then will I attempt to present the ethical principles from which I have proceeded in my reckoning with Stalinism.

There have been recurrent polemics among Marxists as to whether a normative ethics is possible from a Marxist standpoint. Had the most talented of them invested as much passion in the development of a Marxist ethics, it would surely be in a stronger position than it is today.

In the official Marxism of the Third International, ethics devoid of analysis and explication remains a legitimate and even obligatory part of Marxist philosophy. Stalinism has contributed a flood of publications devoted to "ethics," for the ruling statist class has need of a moralistic ideology. Not even after Stalin's death was there a real reorientation; instead, there was merely an improvement in the technical quality of officially accepted ethics in the USSR and certain other countries of the "socialist camp."[57] A radical critique of this brand of ethics, which is based on the *Moral Code of the Builder of Communism in the USSR,* is, in my judgment, an essential precondition for the development of Marxist ethics.

The opponents of a normative ethics in Marxism construe Marx's thought in either a *positivistic* or a *Hegelian* manner. Both, as a rule, hold up *Kantian* ethics as a negative model. These three elements will define the course of the discussion that follows.

Prevalent in the Marxism of the Second International was the understanding of Marx's teaching as a value-neutral science of the "natural laws" of the movement of society and history. In the first part of this book it was asserted that naturalistic-economistic determinism comprises only one dimension of Marx's work. There I presented and analyzed primarily the synchronic aspect of that dimension: the relationship between the economic base and the social superstructure. But there is in addition a diachronic aspect which is also relevant to a consideration of Marxist ethics, that which asserts the inevitability of the succession of socio-economic formations in the sequence, slaveholding — feudalism — capitalism — socialism/communism.

It is natural that a normative ethics should be totally alien to those who approach Marx from the standpoint of naturalistic-economistic determinism. If there exist laws of history which define the fall of capitalism and the future of socialism with "iron necessity," then there is truly no sense in *ethically obligating* people to struggle for socialism. Why should a science of historical inevitability, according to which people are capable at best of accelerating or slowing down the course of history but not of changing it, have any interest at all in affirming ethical ideals, goals, values, and norms? An ethics for which freedom is the recognition of historical necessity, and for which obligation is the stimulating of that necessity, is devoid of any true justification.

Marxists who wish to develop a normative ethics have no choice but to liberate themselves from naturalistic-economistic determinism. A theory for which socialism is a possibility and tendency instead of an inevitability leaves sufficient room for human influence and accordingly for the assignment of normative values to human actions and responsibilities for it.

In arguments against normative ethics, the following passage from Marx is commonly cited: "Communism is not for us a *state of affairs* which is to be established, an *ideal* to which reality [will] have to adjust itself. We call communism the *real* movement which abolishes the present state of things."[58] Here we are not dealing with some "awkward" formulation, as it appears to the proponents of Marxist ethics, but rather with a statement that is in full agreement with naturalistic-economistic determinism. If communism flows from historical inevitability, then it really makes no sense to tout it as an ideal. Only the following type of formulation would correspond to Marx's more moderate determinism: Communism is not for us *primarily* a state of affairs which is to be established, nor *primarily* an ideal to which reality will have to adjust itself. We call communism *above all* the real movement which abolishes the present state of things.

In Marx's time there was very good reason to establish socialism and communism as firmly as possible as a science. Thus Marx decisively criticized the utopian socialists. When, however, one takes into consideration the fact that those who have struggled in the name of Marxism have always been motivated by the *ideals* of freedom, social equality, justice, and so on, then Marxists must be severely reproached for having done so little toward an *ethical justification* of socialism and communism. To be sure, reality has often been perceived in the light of unreal, abstract, and arbitrary ideals. This is a characteristic of *idealogy* as a type of *ideology*. But Marxist theory and the Marxist movement can commit themselves to the realization of real, concrete, and historically grounded ideals.

There is another argument that is used against normative ethics in Marxism. In the *Manifesto of the Communist Party* Marx and Engels remark in passing that communism will lead to the transcending of morality. Lenin eliminated this doctrinal obstacle to Marxist ethics by asserting that morality will play a mediating regulatory role in the classless society. This deepened the split among Marxists between those who predicted the withering away of morality and others who anticipated the flowering of a universal human morality.

Let us assume for the moment that the former were right. Yet the conviction that this would prove the impossibility and superfluousness of Marxist ethics is groundless. For not even they deny that morality will still last for a very long time. Must morality, then, really remain unexamined and unvalued by Marxists?

The belief that morality will wither away is connected to the absolute-utopian component of Marx's vision of communism.[59] Marx, that is to say, defined communism on occasion as a society in which the contradictions between humanism and naturalism, human essence and existence, freedom and necessity, self-affirmation and objectification, individual and species, etc. will disappear. Proceeding from this, many Marxists have believed that communism will establish a definitive identity between being and need. The latter, in their view, even when in moral form, represents an expression of "abstract" and "mediated" sociability, as well as "apparent" humanity, and thus a form of alienation. They find support for this, for instance, in Marx's critique of Stirner: "He believes that in communist society there can be talk of 'obligations' and 'interests,' of two mutually complementary sides of the contradiction which belongs solely to bourgeois society. . . ."[60]

These absolute-utopian moments reveal that Marx did not totally free himself from the influence of Hegel as the philosopher of the absolute idea, the self-development of which culminates in the identity of being and need. At such moments Marx's dialectic, non-idealistic as it may be, is virtually transformed into a peculiar philosophical identity of its own. If *perfect* communism were to mean not only the end of "prehistory" but in its own way the end of history as well, the advent of communism would entail the irrevocable triumph of the absence of dialectics.

People become alienated only in heteronomous moral systems or dimensions, while in autonomous morality they fulfill their humanity and sociability in the most immediate and concrete manner. If communism is imagined as a planetary society, it will be possible to anticipate above all that it will be more complex, not more simple, than previous societies. If even autonomously held moral norms were to cease to exist in it, how would relations among people be regulated? All that we know about man and history demonstrates that not a single society is able to function without a normative minimum. Thus the burden of proof falls not on the opponents of the absolute utopia of the withering away of morality, but on its advocates. To be sure, a free society might surrender far more interpersonal relationships to spontaneity than ever before. Only when the issue is pre-formulated and limited in this way does the idea of the "moral anarchism" (or even "immoralism") of communist society merit serious consideration.

*   *   *

In the history of human thought, extreme positions have sometimes generated reactions in the form of other extreme positions. It was the fate of positivistic Marxism to find itself quickly confronted with a competitor in the ethical socialism of the neo-Kantians. Then it was demanded that Marx's teaching be supplemented by Kantian ethics. There are several reasons why such compounds were bound to disintegrate.

The first is quite obvious: the unbridgeable anthropological and epistemological contradictions between the teachings of Kant and Marx. The dualism of the noumenal and the phenomenal, as well as of the *a priori* and the *a posteriori,* cannot be made consistent with Marx's thought.

If naturalistic-economistic determinism is indeed intolerant of the notion of ethical need, at least of the *a priori* kind of ethical need found in Kant, then how do things stand with regard to Marx's tempered determinism and Kant's ethics? Kant's work is characterized by a sharp dualism—need, motive, subjectivity, individuality, and privacy on the one hand; and being, consequence, objectivity, sociability, and institutionality on the other. Solely the former participate in the constitution of morality, whereas the latter fall into the sphere of legality. Nevertheless this is no ordinary motivational ethics which simply proclaims the consequences of human actions irrelevant to the moral sphere. The sole acceptable motive for Kant's ethics is a feeling of respect for moral law, while other incentives—which in any other ethics would be considered moral—are for Kant legal rather than moral.

Hegel's critique of Kant's view of morality had a strong impact on Marx. Totally committed to radical social change, one of Marx's first orders of business was to familiarize himself with what Kant had advanced in the field of legality. Since he wished to ground his revolutionary theory in the inclinations, aspirations, and interests of real people (more precisely, the proletariat), Marx found Kant's rigoristic and formalistic ethics of "pure" need and "pure" will to be alien to him.

It is no exaggeration to say that Kant represents the most extreme standpoint in the history of ethics in terms of constructing an ideal model of moralism and ethicism. Nevertheless some Marxists, influenced by Hegel, take Kant's understanding of morality and ethics as the paradigm of the moral and ethical position. For precisely this reason they react negatively to the very mention of ethics in Marxism. But it is utterly groundless to believe that the Hegelian and Marxist critique of Kant's concept of practical reason vitiates the essence of *any* morality and *any* ethics.

Lest these critical remarks on Kant seem unforgiveably one-sided, it is necessary to add that with his categorical imperative he made a valuable contribution to humanistic ethics which must be taken into account by Marxist ethical theorists. Kant's message still resounds to the present day: "Act so that you treat humanity, whether in your own person or in that of another, always as an end and never as a means only."

The weaknesses of Kant's ethics pointed Marxists toward Hegel, who aspired to eliminate the dichotomies that had been characteristic of philosophy up to his time. Nowhere, probably, where they more obvious than in Kant. Hegel believed that these internal contradictions and limitations of "morality" were overcome in what he called *Sittlichkeit*. Their attention being directed preeminently toward socio-historical problems, Marxists were naturally impressed with this shift of philosophical attention from need, motive, subjectivity, individuality, and privacy to being, consequences, objectivity, sociability, and institutionality.

But some of them foresaw that Hegel's *Sittlichkeit,* instead of effectively serving as a real synthesis, was in fact just the opposite. With their exaggerated Hegelian bias and immoderate anti-Kantianism, such Marxists, in analyzing and evaluating human activity, lose sight of motives related, for example, to efficiency. Let us also mention here the conformist potential of Hegel's thought. Guided by his negative reaction to the "capriciousness" of the individual's moral judgment, Hegel interceded in favor of social institutions, and above all of the state in which the unity of need and being is allegedly manifested. In short, instead of expanding the domain of ethics, Hegel unjustifiably dissolved it into a critique of morals in general and in social philosophy (state and law). Insofar as Hegel's system in fact contains no ethics, it is not surprising that there is no place for ethics in Hegelian Marxism.

* * *

There are many ways of misconstruing the essence of Marx's thought. One of the most frequent and reliable ways of doing so is to overlook the specific quality of Marx's linguistic and conceptual instrumentation deriving from the Hegelian school. In this type of philosophizing the dualism of factual and normative (value) statements, which is otherwise characteristic of the Kantian and neopositivist traditions alike, is absent.

For Hegel the *real* (or true) is that which presently *exists* which is in unity with its *essence.* This unity, rather than being merely given, is of a latent, tendentious, and processual character. For Hegel and many of his followers, that is to say, one and the same judgment (about reality) performs both functions which for the Kantians and neopositivists are covered in strictly separate judgments.

Regardless of what the Hegelians may think, however, this does not eliminate the old problem of making logical distinctions and relationships between cognition and normation (valuation); instead, it merely poses it in a different form. Hegel, that is to say, shifted the problem from the context of the relationship of two types of judgments to that of the relationship of two aspects of the same judgment. As "the existing"—contrary to Hegel's belief—bears within itself more than one possibility, the question of which of them *ought* to be realized in order that the existing may correspond to its essence is crucial. What is the answer, if not normation (valuation)?

Gajo Petrović rightly insists that the path to understanding Marx leads through Hegel. He maintains that my effort to demonstrate the possibility of and need for a Marxist ethics is doomed to failure from the outset because it proceeds from a lack of understanding of Marx's thought:

> The root of this failure lies in the fact that he, like others who have wished to establish a Marxist ethics, operates in the dualism between fact and value, or rather between factual and value judgments. To be sure he attempts to mitigate this dualism by asserting that Marx did not draw an unbridgeable distinction "between cognitive and value statements." Nevertheless he does not arrive at the hypothesis that in addition to and prior to "cognitive" and "value" statements there could be *essential* "statements," which make assertions about neither existing facticity nor only imagined ideals but about the *essential possibility of human being.* He also does not arrive at the idea that the descriptive statements of science and the normative statements of ethics perhaps are only a derivative and alienated form of those judgments that adequately approximate truth.[61]

Marx's goal, of course, was not to make either "purely" factual or "purely" normative statements. I might remark in passing that while Marx's thought indeed leaves no room for the dichotomy of fact and norm (value), at the same time it does contain an element of positivism in that it takes natural science as the model for all science and seeks out "natural laws" of socio-historical movement.

Marx certainly does make use of categories that often unify cognition and valuation (normation), such as man's generic being, human need, alienation, reification, commodity fetishism, exploitation, surplus value, and so on. He consciously avoids the most general and substantively empty statements using "good," "correct," "ought," etc. as predicates. Whether we call Marx's statements that unify cognition and valuation (normation) "essential" or something else is not so important as whether we affirm their significance and the problems that they conceal.

In his essence, man, says Petrović, "is not only what he is *factually* in his alienation, but also what he *can* and *ought to* become."[62] And it turns out that "essential statements" contain a normative aspect, since they speak not of some human "potential" but rather of that which *ought* to be realized. In these statements it is obviously no "real form of human being"[63] that attains expression, but rather one which *ought* to be supported. And this means, moreover, that the very same question is posed with regard to "essential" statements as was left unanswered in connection with Hegel's judgments about "reality."

Philosophers have not ceased to cross swords over the nature of the transition from "is" (and "can") to "ought": this divides them into cognitivists and anti-cognitivists. While the former assert that the transition is of a *logical* character, the latter persuasively deny that this is the case. While this logical problem was not of interest to Marx, it is easy to show that his *implicit* convictions caused him, like Hegel, to be a cognitivist.

Why does Gajo Petrović operate on the (tacit) assumption that Marx had to be an anti-cognitivist and even that he would have had to make "purely" normative (value) statements if we are to be able to speak of an ethical component of his thought? Not only is it the case that there is such a thing as cognitivist ethics; indeed such ethics have dominated the history of philosophy. Where is it written, moreover, that ethics must be built on the Kantian model? Kantian ethics is not in the slightest "traditional," for the history of ethics is far more replete with thinkers who did not believe in the existence of a chasm between being and need.

Nor is it unimportant that anti-cognitivism today is incomparably less exclusive than it was two or three decades ago. Nearly no one of any competence denies nowadays that value-normative statements have a cognitive dimension as well. To be sure, the polemic with the cognitivists continues, but over the primacy of the non-cognitive as opposed to the cognitive dimension of these statements, as well as over the nature of the logical relationship between those dimensions.[64]

To bring this discussion into focus, I would explicitly delimit two issues. The first relates to Marx's (implicit) cognitivistic *meta-ethical* conception, and the second to the *ethical* component of his thought.

Marx's cognitivism is insupportable — not because he actually makes "essential" judgments instead of "purely" cognitive and "purely" value (normative) ones, but because he tacitly assumes that the total content of these "essential" judgments follows *with logical necessity* from corresponding *acts of cognition,* whereas in fact their content is also defined by Marx's revolutionary-humanistic *commitment.*

However one might define and evaluate Marx's (implicit) meta-ethical viewpoint, it is indisputable that his thought also has a value-normative, ethical component. This component must be taken as a stimulus, both deliberately and critically, by every Marxist who seeks to construct a normative ethics.

Since he knows that Marx's "essential" judgments contain value-normative moments, Petrović increasingly restricts his original thesis in the course of his exposition. He begins with the intention of showing that a Marxist ethics is generally incapable of being established, and finishes with the conclusion that "in the framework of Marxism ethics is not possible as an independent philosophical discipline."[65] As Marxism by its nature is not generally amenable to being divided up into disciplines—which, to be sure, Petrović himself says can be useful in academic instruction—Petrović does allow that what he has said regarding ethics holds equally for ontology, epistemology, anthropology, etc.

But there are limits to everything. Marxism is a whole, but in no case is it a whole that cannot be articulated and dissected. Furthermore, I believe it is most important for Marxists to attempt to study and resolve normative-ethical problems and that whether they group these questions and answers in a special discipline is a totally secondary matter. But there is no question, of course, that in doing so the Marxist must approach moral issues, just as any others, from a *revolutionary-humanistic* standpoint.

* * *

The real opposite of *revolutionary* humanism is *moralistic* (ethicistic), rather than *moral* (ethical), humanism, although the critics of Marxist ethics may imagine otherwise. Whenever they speak of morality and ethics they automatically think of moralism and ethicism—but on what grounds? There is not a single decent argument for drawing this identity, not even on the assumption that the revolutionary position were to logically or factually exclude the moral viewpoint. Perhaps it is also not insignificant that Marxist revolutionaries most commonly feel a strong need to justify their undertakings in a moral sense as well as in others. The defense of the October Revolution against Kautsky's attacks is just one example.

The moralizer, above all, confronts people with a conception of how they ought to be, while the point is to make radical changes in the social conditions in which they live. The Marxist approach to moral consciousness is fundamentally realistic because it is based on the awareness that consciousness is itself conditioned by social existence. The naive moralist entertains hopes that people will be changed in a fundamental way—say, that they will no longer treat one another primarily as means—while their socio-economic system remains just as it is. This is why Marx appealed to man not simply to cease behaving like an oppressed, degraded, abandoned, despised being, but to eliminate the social conditions that make him such a being.

This *systemic-institutional* approach is characteristic of Marxism as a whole, and this applies to its ethics as well. Not only is it possible for Marxist revolutionaries to feel a *moral* obligation to transform the class social system and its institutions; this is what actually happens. It is not idle to repeat, however, that commitment to the revolutionary position does not necessarily entail the choice of violence as a means of radical change.

138 *In Search of Democracy in Socialism*

Care must be taken lest the systemic-institutional approach slide into reification and superdeterminism—as if social systems and institutions are not composed of people, their interpersonal relations and activities, and as if these systems and institutions unilaterally determine their behavior. In reality this is only a framework that leaves a great deal of latitude for individual and group choices, decisions, positions, and commitments—including those of a moral nature.

With this there are associated two types of errors. The first is moralistic and occurs when it is believed that it is sufficient for us to rely on moral conscience. But the second is more frequent among Marxists and relates to the guarantees supposedly created by the new social system and new institutions which are to prevent all the most important moral abuses, if not all of them, from taking place. For man has depths which cannot be even touched by any regulatory or oversight mechanisms apart from moral ones. People change, to be sure, with circumstances, but the dimensions and direction of social changes depends upon them and upon how much and in what way they change themselves. In order to transform society in a conscious manner it seems probable that people need to know with what they will be replacing it. Marxists have always paid dearly for believing that in this respect moral conscience and ethics have nothing to say.

It is true that while the moralist places his faith in the transformation of individuals, the Marxist places his in collective action directed toward changing the social state of things. Some Marxists, unfortunately, believe that we must decide between "collective-historical" and "individual-moral" actions. But what of collective-historical efforts simultaneously combined with moral ones? There is surely no hope for a Marxist ethics in the absence of a vigorous revolutionary movement. Marx knew that it is not enough for thought to strive toward reality and that it is essential for reality itself to strive toward thought.

Does it follow from the fact that revolutionary practice is the vehicle of the unity of need and being—what some call the monism of revolutionary practice—that Marxism is irreconcilable in principle with normative ethics? All sorts of things, of course, can be derived from revolutionary practice when it is construed in a transcendental manner. In that case not a single instance of practice *by definition* would be revolutionary unless a total unity of need and being were established within it. Or to put it differently, it would be revolutionary only to the extent that this unity were achieved. Thus it happens that by means of an appropriate *definition* we can resolve the ancient and exceedingly difficult philosophical problem of the logical nature of the relationship between cognition and valuation (normation)! It is in this way that those who unequivocally deny the existence of any normative approach in Marxism themselves end up in normativism.

Nothing is more contrary to Marx's intentions and spirit than to interpret him in such a transcendental manner. Revolutionary practice, for Marx, represents only a *potential* unity of need and being, as well as an *attempt* to establish that unity. In no event was Marx's attitude toward the revolutionary movement positivistic, much less conformist. Regardless of some of his individual formulations, it is undeniable that Marx did have a conception of what the revolutionary movement *ought* to be, not only knowledge of what it really was.

Why have Marxists failed to develop a sense for the *moral* aspect of this normative question regarding the revolutionary movement? Insofar as the revolutionary does act on the basis of moral convictions, is it not better that he be ethically enlightened and evaluated? If it were truly established that ethics is insupportable in Marxism on principle, this would mean that Marxism is powerless to grasp an important aspect of reality and of revolutionary practice.

What is most peculiar is the fact that many Marxist opponents of ethics are otherwise inclined to take every opportunity to stress that there is no revolutionary practice without revolutionary theory (and vice-versa). But why not also hold that there is no revolutionary morality without revolutionary ethics (and vice-versa)? For they know very well whither blind "revolutionary instinct" leads. To the extent that a revolutionary movement rejects ethics, the greater will be its moral tribulations and prospects of losing its way in moral wildernesses.

10. The Dignity of the Revolutionary in the Ethics of Humanistic Reciprocity

The ethics of humanistic reciprocity should hold for the relationship between the revolutionary and his organization with respect to responsibility, loyalty, trust, respect, understanding, allegiance, solidarity, consideration. . . . Those who struggle for a true human community are themselves under an obligation to foster their own community, and this presupposes the existence of the same normative principles for all. In contrast to "party militants," revolutionary comrades-in-arms cannot afford to retreat from this reciprocity. The former are more likely to be used by the party than to participate in its formation.

How, within the framework of humanistic reciprocity, is one to evaluate actions with regard to the difference between objective and subjective meaning and responsibility? The *sine qua non* is that these measures be applied in the same manner and to the same extent to all revolutionaries, "ordinary" as well as those in positions of leadership. In an organization which in addition to *responsibility* is graced by mutual respect, understanding, and consideration — in a word, *friendship* — the actor would be more inclined to take into account as many consequences of his own activity as possible, while his comrades would strive persistently to lay stress on his good intentions in assessing his conduct. Through equal criticism the revolutionaries would develop an enhanced ability to predict the consequences of their own actions and those of others and to rank them far more objectively.

Communist parties have always stressed the need for "human concern." These concerns exist to the extent that there is a real effort to approach human actions with as many conceptual, or at least perceptual, distinctions and nuances as possible. One cannot attend very effectively to human concerns if one loses sight of the boundary, for instance, between various types of objective meaning and between various degrees of objective responsibility. Under these circumstances all manner of consequences—vital and peripheral, foreseen and unforeseen, direct and indirect, foreseeable and unforeseeable—are treated the same. Neither is it terribly important, in such an environment, whether an act was intentional or unavoidable, accidental, a product of the force of circumstance, an act of omission or carelessness, etc. We can speak of anything but concern for the individual when he is constantly having obligations imposed on him, and in this case he will find no understanding, excuse, or justification.

Is it possible to preserve revolutionary discipline and effectiveness with such equality, and so much of it? If one is to reason in a realistic manner, it will have to be acknowledged that under autocracy, driven into illegality and persecuted, those who struggled for communism had no choice but to concentrate and unite their aspirations and actions to the maximum. Those who exclusively ascribe this to the Leninist conception of organization are in error, for in such circumstances it is truly impossible to have democratic elections, controls, rotation, and so forth. Then not even the revolutionary's life is sacrosanct, and each revolutionary has indeed already taken this into account. But in no way can it be shown that readiness to sacrifice one's personal dignity is also essential to the revolutionary's activity.

To be sure, among revolutionaries there has been from time to time a tension between the principle of humanistic mutuality and the need for disciplined action. Of crucial importance, however, is their long-term orientation toward reconciliation of these two demands or toward negation of the former to the advantage of the latter. To carry this argument to its conclusion: any notion of effectiveness which excludes humanistic mutuality speaks of a readiness to seize and hold on to power by any means possible, but not also to bring into being the revolutionary-humanistic goals that one may publicly embrace. It would be wrong to believe that the revolutionary must choose immorality if he wishes to avoid falling victim to naive moralism. In this, unfortunately, Marxist theoreticians will be of little help to him, for they have yet to construct a revolutionary ethics.

From the outset the Bolsheviks knew that their organization would be more centralistic than democratic. They were most fond of comparing revolutionary organization to military organization. Trotsky, for one, uncritically returned to this parallel in 1938 for otherwise obscure reasons in his essay, "Their Morals and Ours."

Stalinization was the source of two extremely consequential deformations. In addition to the legacy of the centralistic division of authority and jurisdiction, there were established various countermeasures, to an examination of which we have devoted an entire section of this book (Part III, Section 8). This was revolutionary discipline distorted into blind oligarchic obedience.

It was no longer possible, moreover, to resign from the party without the most adverse personal consequences. Once it became the ruling party, there was no justification at all for leaving it. Indeed it was easier to leave the party while it was in illegality, although this did create a risk to the party members that remained. In passing we might note that this risk was no greater than that deriving from the danger of police infiltration through the recruitment of new members, for the same type of informing is possible in both situations (admission and resignation). In other words, I am once again suggesting that the revolutionary organization can, in difficult conditions as well, be realistically structured while at the same time remaining capable of guaranteeing a greater degree of individual rights to its members than is commonly supposed possible. Wretched are the fighters for revolutionary-humanistic ideals who would under no conditions dare to break an oath given to their organization!

It is most important to remember that the Bolshevik Party seized power and defended it *before* it became infested with autocracy, inquisitorial behavior between Party members, the constant breaking up of internal "conspiracies," and the like. The longer it stayed in power and the more firmly entrenched it became, the more it became the image and apparition of its erstwhile persecutors.

To think that dignity can be sacrificed for the sake of the revolutionary-humanist cause is an illusion. Dignity is inseparable from the core of the revolutionary's personality, and thus from the cause for which he fights as well. To act in a contrary manner is to render the revolutionary cause void of the dignity of those who struggle in its behalf and to misconstrue such a dehumanized value as an intrinsic value to which all other values serve as means. Only if he is persistent in his vigilance concerning dignity, his own and that of his comrades-in-arms, will the revolutionary be in a position to contribute to the realm of value.

In agreeing to the sacrifice of his dignity the revolutionary brings into question the moral worth of his personality and thereby the moral value of his sacrifice. For man is the bearer and realizer of value. Here we are not speaking, moreover, of an ordinary *surplus sacrifice* but of a sacrifice which devalues the very act of sacrifice. There is no realistic ethics of violent revolution — inevitable and justified under certain circumstances — that is capable of totally eliminating the need for *revolutionary suspension of certain aspects of morality*. But dignity is a moral value which the revolutionary imperils solely at the cost of his own humanistic goals.

If revolutionary sacrifices must be employed to the end of creating conditions for the flourishing of the human personality, then these sacrifices cannot be effective without conscious *personalistic self-restraint*. In this respect the revolutionary's dignity is an absolutely necessary minimum condition. In this the revolutionary must, of course, be sensitive to the need to subordinate a certain degree of personal freedom to the collective effort. Thus his dignity is not egoistic or isolated in a vacuum, but is rather comradely and solidaristic.

The organization of revolutionaries must be the harbinger and initiator of human emancipation. In this connection I would refer to Marx's thoughts on the community of revolutionary proletarians:

> It follows from all we have been saying up till now that the communal relationship into which the individuals of a class entered, and which was determined by their common interests over against a third party, was always a community to which these individuals belonged only as average individuals, only insofar as they lived within the conditions of their class—a relationship in which they participated not as individuals but as members of a class. With the *community of revolutionary proletarians,* on the other hand, who take their conditions of existence and those of all members of society under their control, it is just the reverse; *it is as individuals that the individuals participate in it.*[66]

An organization of humiliated people has no revolutionary-humanist future. What kind of "concern for man" can there be unless his dignity is taken into account? Occasionally it will be argued that the revolutionary party's program is unrealizable. It would be a dangerous illusion if the unpreparedness of its members to sacrifice their human pride were to be thought of as a plausible explanation of this circumstance in any sense. One cannot be worthy of the dignity of associating with the revolutionary-humanist cause unless one possesses dignity oneself. Therefore the preservation of personal dignity is an obligation not only toward oneself but toward the revolution as well.

Many thinkers insist that under certain conditions the individual has the right and duty to engage in civil disobedience. Why do communists speak immeasurably less about the revolutionary's right and duty to oppose his own organization when he is convinced that its activity is not consistent with revolutionary-humanist ideals?

It is painful to recall Trotsky's words at the Thirteenth Congress of the Bolshevik Party in 1923: "None of us wishes to be right against his party, none of us can be right against his party. The party is always right in the final analysis because it represents the sole historical means of the proletariat for realizing its fundamental tasks." What does it matter that Trotsky shortly thereafter changed his thinking and conduct when innumerable communists had already been trained to absolutize the party?

In the eyes of the Stalinized communist the party was much more than a form of revolutionary practice. It was above the party member; the proletariat was above the proletarian; the revolution above the revolutionary; history above people: and in the final analysis the party was above all. Among Stalinists the principle of party-mindedness was incomparably more meaningful than that of revolution-mindedness. Those who have written about this period very often cite the metaphor of the *revolution which devours its own children*. But I see before me another picture as well—the revolution which *abases its own children*.

To avoid this it is not sufficient to have specific institutional guarantees and the ability to render transparent the Stalinist distorted consciousness. A corresponding moral self-consciousness and sensitivity is necessary as well. Stalinist abasement is the exact opposite of Marx's Promethean ideal. There was nothing for which Marx had greater contempt than servility. The target of his criticism was not solely exploitation, but abasement as well. Marx's *"categorical imperative to overthrow all those conditions* in which man is an abased, enslaved, abandoned, contemptible being"[67] must hold before all else for communists themselves and their interpersonal relationships.

One can only wish that the legacy of Stalinism were so widespread and well appreciated that communists might, from the very first, honor the principle: *Do not treat personal dignity as a means in the revolutionary effort!* The transcendence of the realm of necessity by the realm of freedom—that ultimate goal of Marxist strugglers—cannot even be imagined without the establishment of the realm of man as an end in himself.

NOTES TO PART THREE

1. Antonije Isaković, "Revolucija je otvoreni žrtvenik" [Revolution is an Open Sacrificial Altar], *Književne novine,* October 16, 1971.
2. Cited in Victor A. Kravchenko, *I Chose Freedom: The Personal and Political Life of a Soviet Official* (New York: Scribner's, 1946), p. 275.
3. *The New York Times,* May 26, 1971.
4. As cited in *Borba,* March 9, 1972.
5. Zamyatin, *My* [We].
6. Milan Kundera, *Šala* [The Joke] (Zagreb: 1969), p. 52; see *La plaisanterie* (Paris: Gallimard, 1968).
7. Aldous Huxley, *Brave New World* (New York: Bantam, 1958), p. 26.
8. Maurice Merleau-Ponty, *Humanism and Terror,* trans. John O'Neill (Boston: Beacon, 1969), p. 144.
9. Robert Conquest, *The Great Terror: Stalin's Purge of the Thirties,* rev. ed. (New York: Macmillan, 1973), p. 18; my emphasis—S.S.
10. György Lukács, "Taktika i etika" [Tactics and Ethics], as cited in the collection *Etika i politika* (Zagreb: 1972), pp. 32 ff.
11. Merleau-Ponty, p. 70; my emphasis—S.S.
12. *Ibid.,* pp. 43-44; my emphasis—S.S.
13. *Ibid.,* p. 43; my emphasis—S.S.
14. *Ibid.,* p. xxxiii; my emphasis—S.S.
15. *Ibid.,* p. xxxix; my emphasis—S.S.
16. *Ibid.,* p. 42; my emphasis—S.S.
17. Albert Camus, *The Rebel* (New York: Vintage, 1967), p. 242.
18. *Ibid.,* p. 241.
19. Merleau-Ponty, p. 69.

20. Karl Marx, *Capital,* "Preface to the First German Edition" (New York: International Publishers, 1967), vol. I, p. 10; my emphasis—S.S.
21. Merleau-Ponty, p. 44.
22. Maurice Merleau-Ponty, *Eloge de la philosophie* (Paris: 1953), p. 11; with the exception of the word "simultaneously," all emphases are my own—S.S.
23. Sartre, *Search for a Method,* p. 89.
24. *Ibid.,* p. 90.
25. Weber, p. 123.
26. Merleau-Ponty, *Humanism and Terror,* p. xxxiv; my emphasis—S.S.
27. Dankwart A. Rustow, "The Study of Leadership," in *Philosophers and Kings: Studies in Leadership,* ed. Dankwart A. Rustow (New York: George Brazillier, 1970), p. 28.
28. Merleau-Ponty, *Humanism and Terror,* p. 26; my emphasis—S.S.
29. *Ibid.,* p. 27; my emphasis—S.S.
30. *Ibid.,* p. 28; my emphasis—S.S.
31. *Ibid.,* p. 31; my emphasis—S.S.
32. *Ibid.,* p. 43; my emphasis—S.S.
33. *Ibid.,* p. 82 and ff.
34. *Ibid.,* p. xv; my emphasis—S.S.
35. *Ibid.,* pp. 1–2; my emphasis—S.S.
36. *Ibid.,* p. xxxiii.
37. *Ibid.,* p. xv.
38. Andrey Platonov, "Makar sumnjalo" [Although With Doubts], from the anthology *Tajanstveni covek* [The Mysterious Man] (Belgrade: 1968), p. 52; my emphasis—S.S.
39. Cf. Marx, "Economic-Philosophical Manuscripts," in *The Marx-Engels Reader,* p. 72 and ff.
40. Kundera, *op. cit.*
41. Albert Camus, *The Myth of Sisyphus.*
42. George Orwell, *Animal Farm* (New York: Harcourt, Brace, and Co., 1946), p. 21.
43. Leon Trotsky, *My Life* (New York: Scribner's, 1930), pp. 529 ff.
44. Carl Landauer, *European Socialism* (Berkeley: University of California Press, 1959), vol. II, pp. 1241–1242.
45. Enrica Collotti Pischel, *Kineska revolucija* [The Chinese Revolution] (Belgrade: 1970), p. 36.
46. See *Istorijski arhiv KPJ* [Historical Archive of the Communist Party of Yugoslavia], vol. II, p. 465.
47. Georg Lukács, *History and Class Consciousness: Studies in Marxist Dialectics,* trans. Rodney Livingstone (London: Merlin Press, 1971), p. xxx.
48. *Ibid.,* p. xxxviii.
49. "Bulgakov's Letter to the Soviet Government," *Dissent,* May–June 1969, pp. 271–272.
50. Antonio Gramsci, "Notes on Economics," from *Historical Materialism and the Philosophy of Benedetto Croce.* See *Il materialismo storico e la filosofia di Benedetto Croce* (Rome: Riuniti, 1971).
51. Zamyatin, *My.*
52. *Ibid.*
53. In *The God That Failed,* ed. Richard Crossman (New York: Bantam, 1952), p. 144; my emphasis—S.S.
54. Karl Marx, *The Holy Family,* as cited from the Serbo-Croatian edition of the Marx-Engels *Works (Dela),* vol. 5, p. 157.
55. Karl Marx, "The Eighteenth Brumaire of Louis Bonaparte," in *The Marx-Engels Reader,* pp. 597–598; my emphasis—S.S.
56. "Farewell Oration," from *Besede* [Orations] (Belgrade: 1966), p. 102.
57. It is precisely this ethics which is endorsed by H. J. Sandkuhler in his introductory and bibliographical contributions to the anthology *Marxismus und Ethik: Texte zum neukantianischen*

Sozialismus, which he coedited with R. de la Vega for Suhrkamp (1970 and 1974). In this context it is quite logical that he should direct his wrath against anti-Stalinist Marxists. He also devotes a good deal of space to an assault on my previous book, *Between Ideals and Reality.* Insofar as what is at issue here is a quite ordinary ideological-political attack rather than a rationally argued theoretical critique, I feel myself under no obligation to respond.

58. Marx, "German Ideology," in *The Marx-Engels Reader,* p. 162.
59. I have written about the tension between the absolute-utopian and relative-utopian components of Marx's concept of communism in the second chapter of *Between Ideals and Reality.*
60. Marx, "The German Ideology," as cited in the Serbo-Croatian *Dela,* vol. 6, p. 170.
61. Gajo Petrović, *Filozofija i revolucija* [Philosophy and Revolution] (Zagreb: 1971), p. 204; with the exception of the first "essential," all emphases are my own—S.S.
62. *Ibid.,* p. 202; my emphasis—S.S.
63. *Ibid.,* p. 199.
64. I would direct the reader with an interest in the dispute between the cognitivists and anticognitivists to my first book, *Savremena metaetika* [Contemporary Meta-Ethics] (Belgrade: 1964), in which I laid out my own moderate anticognitivist position.
65. Petrović, p. 202.
66. Marx, "German Ideology," in *The Marx Engels Reader,* pp. 197–198; my emphasis—S.S.
67. Marx, "Contribution to the Critique of Hegel's *Philosophy of Right: Introduction,"* in *The Marx-Engels Reader,* p. 60.